# JUDGEMENT OF
# THE PHARAOH

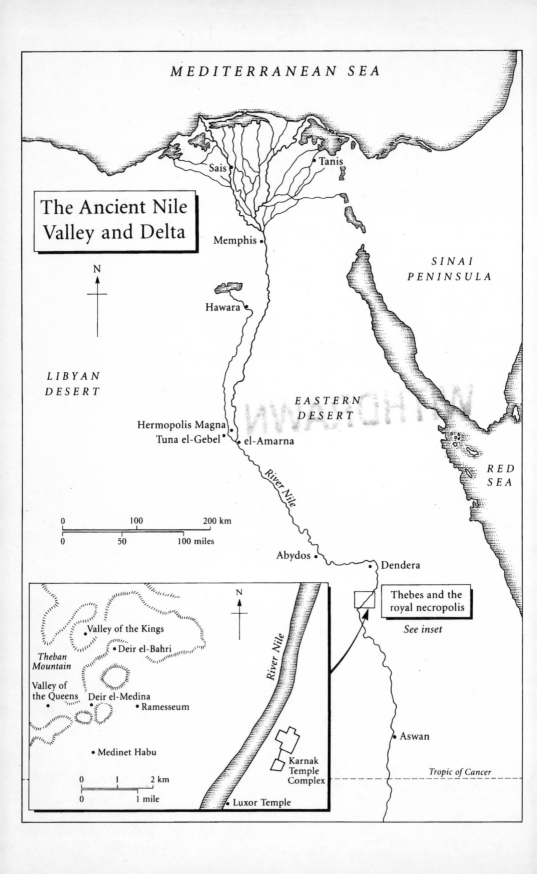

MEDITERRANEAN SEA

The Ancient Nile
Valley and Delta

N

Sais

Tanis

Memphis

SINAI
PENINSULA

Hawara

LIBYAN
DESERT

EASTERN
DESERT

Hermopolis Magna
Tuna el-Gebel • el-Amarna

River Nile

RED
SEA

0        100        200 km
0     50     100 miles

Abydos •        • Dendera

Thebes and the
royal necropolis

*See inset*

**Inset: Thebes and the royal necropolis**

N

Valley of the Kings

• Deir el-Bahri

*Theban
Mountain*

River Nile

Valley of
the Queens

Deir el-Medina
• Ramesseum

• Medinet Habu

Karnak
Temple
Complex

0     1     2 km
0          1 mile

• Luxor Temple

Aswan

*Tropic of Cancer*

# JUDGEMENT OF THE PHARAOH

*Crime and Punishment in Ancient Egypt*

Joyce Tyldesley

Weidenfeld & Nicolson

LONDON

First published in Great Britain in 2000
by Weidenfeld & Nicolson

© 2000 Joyce Tyldesley

The moral right of Joyce Tyldesley to be identified as the
author of this work has been asserted in accordance with
the Copyright, Designs and Patents Act of 1988.

Plates 1–3 are reproduced courtesy of Robert Partridge, The Ancient Egypt
Picture Library and plates 4–9 courtesy of S. Snape. Plate 10 of the X-ray of Tutankhamen's
skull is reproduced by kind permission of the Department of Human Anatomy,
University of Liverpool.

A CIP catalogue record for this book
is available from the British Library.

ISBN 0 297 64669 9

Typeset by Deltatype Ltd, Birkenhead, Merseyside
Printed in Great Britain by Clays Ltd, St Ives plc


Weidenfeld & Nicolson

The Orion Publishing Group Ltd
Orion House
5 Upper Saint Martin's Lane
London, WC2H 9EA

For Professor Ken Kitchen

# Contents

# Preface

When I started this book I was well aware that the image of ancient Egypt as a land of constant happiness and contentment had sunk deep into the popular imagination, but I was somewhat taken aback when a distinguished colleague, who shall remain nameless, queried my choice of subject: 'Crime and punishment in ancient Egypt – surely there wasn't any?' Of course there was. Egypt, whatever her scribes and artists would have us believe, was by no means the perfect society. This book represents my attempt to correct a one-sided view of a civilisation that, while undeniably pleasant for many, nevertheless had its darker side.

After a brief introduction, I have divided the book into three main sections dealing respectively with the administration of the law; crimes against the state; and civil or private offences, including the judgement of the dead. As far as possible I have used contemporary documents and cases to allow the Egyptians to speak for themselves. As I am conscious that the egyptologist's habit of littering his or her writings with copious endnotes is irritating to the general reader, I have used endnotes solely to provide full references to the texts I have quoted in free translation. Many of these references are to scholarly works difficult for the lay-reader to obtain; this is regrettable but unavoidable. The bibliography at the end of the book includes

1

more accessible publications, with priority given to books written in English.

I would like to thank everyone who has helped in the production of this book – you know who you are!

JOYCE TYLDESLEY
Bolton 1999

# LAW IN ACTION

Great is Justice, its effectiveness endures,
Unchallenged since the time of Osiris.[1]

The idyllic daily rhythm of dynastic Egypt is preserved in a series
of beautifully decorated private tombs on the west bank of the
River Nile at Thebes. Here, in the tomb of the official Sennedjem,
we see the deceased and his wife as they toil side by side in the
fields. Their work is enjoyable rather than taxing and the couple
appear relaxed and even happy as they gather their crops. In the
not too far distant tomb of the vizier Rekhmire we are treated to
more vigorous scenes of prosperity, pomp and circumstance. We
can watch with Rekhmire as craftsmen labour to his command, as
a sumptuous banquet is prepared, and even as the king himself is
crowned. Such scenes of urban affluence and rural tranquillity are
by no means the sole preserve of the New Kingdom dead. A series
of near-identical images stretches back through time to the Old
Kingdom tombs, built many centuries before Sennedjem's death,
that surround the royal pyramids of Giza and Sakkara.

Just occasionally we are allowed a glimpse of a less than ideal
world which helps to break up the bland perfection of the more
orthodox tableaux. Nothing too disturbing is shown. An ugly or
deformed servant may be introduced to impart an element of
comic relief. Peasants, having refused to pay their taxes, are

flogged for their pains. A nobleman, displeased with his subordinate, watches impassively as the offender is tied to a post and beaten with a stick. None of these disruptions to harmony are serious, and peace is soon restored. The observer is invited to sympathise with the tomb-owner, to smile at the aberrations and to admire anew the well-ordered world where the élite control and protect the masses and everyone lives content with his or her lot beneath the ever-smiling Egyptian sun.

Had the Egyptians truly discovered the secret of the perpetually perfect society? Are the dissatisfactions and inequalities which lead to crime a modern development? Of course not. Dynastic Egypt was a vibrant society well-grounded in economic realism. The images that decorate the tomb walls of Thebes and Giza should properly be read as a gigantic piece of propaganda – a view of life as it should be lived, seen from the viewpoint of the upper classes who wished to replicate their idealised earthly existence beyond death. These scenes repeat one particular story, a story that to a large extent excludes society's unfortunates: the very old, the very young, the very poor, the sick, the maimed, and the mentally disturbed.

The same bias must be recognised in the monumental inscriptions carved to celebrate the glories, and never the seamier side, of Egyptian life. A king might make a passing reference to social problems, but only as a prelude to explaining how he personally has corrected the situation. No monarch would waste valuable wall-space on a 'warts and all' account of daily life; no one would be interested in the complaints and sufferings of the individual. This is entirely to be expected. Few, if any, governments choose to highlight the failures of their régime, and the Egyptian kings had more reason than most to perpetuate the image of a glorious reign for they believed that writing could convey a magical truth. To commit a statement to hieroglyphs was in many ways to make that statement come true.

In fact, as we might expect, life for the vast majority of the population was far removed from the bucolic prosperity of the tomb walls, and only a privileged few were ever able to enjoy in full the fruits of their land's fertility. Throughout the dynastic age a rigidly stratified social structure ensured that Egypt's enormous wealth was controlled by the top five or six per cent of the population. At the very peak of the social pyramid came the king, or Pharaoh, an all-powerful, semi-divine being who owned the entire land and its produce, including the people. Below him came the educated élite, a tight-knit, inter-related group of several hundred families who governed the country on their king's behalf, acting as priests and administrators and receiving as their reward a share in the king's riches. With this wealth came responsibility, and the élite had a well-understood moral – but not legal – duty to care for those less fortunate than themselves. These upper classes, the builders of stone tombs, carvers of inscriptions and hoarders of golden funerary artefacts, have left behind enough evidence to allow us to reconstruct their lives with a fair degree of accuracy.

Beneath the élite, in ever-increasing numbers, came the educated upper-middle classes, the skilled artisans and, finally, the million-plus unskilled peasants who made up the vast bulk of the population. Egypt was a fertile country little given to natural disasters. As long as the River Nile functioned correctly she offered a life with little risk of drought or starvation. Nevertheless, the work of the peasants who supported the economy was long, hard and dull. Tied to the land, illiterate and far removed from the bounty that the gods lavished on their social superiors, the farm labourers were regarded as work units rather than as people. As such, during the months of flooding when work on the fields was impossible, they might be conscripted at random to fight in Pharaoh's army or to labour on one of Egypt's magnificent civil projects, the waterways, earthworks and monuments designed to glorify Pharaoh's name. These peasants, so important to the ancient economy, are today largely invisible, their mud-brick architecture long since crumbled to dust and their names entirely forgotten.

The towns and cities of the middle classes, too, have largely disappeared, although we are fortunate in having a handful of purpose-built sites which have survived in relatively good condition. Of utmost importance in our understanding of Egyptian justice is Deir el-Medina, the village occupied for some five centuries by the artisans who worked in the royal cemeteries of Thebes. This site has yielded a wealth of documentation, preserving the portrait of a crowded, claustrophobic and inbred village where neighbourly quarrels soon escalated into fierce feuds variously requiring the intervention of the family, the local court or even the divine oracle of the deified Amenhotep I. Their proximity to, and intimate knowledge of, the gold-filled tombs of the kings and queens was a constant temptation to the workmen of Deir el-Medina, a temptation that some were unable to resist.

History shows that the development of the state and the development of crime have a depressing tendency to go hand in hand; it seems that in all societies avarice and greed escalate with increasing wealth and social complexity. The Egyptian record certainly provides clear evidence for a trend of ever-increasing crime levels and progressively brutal punishments as the dynasties progress, with lawlessness peaking at times of social unrest and subsiding as authority is once again restored. As Egypt's wealth steadily increased, the New Kingdom Egyptian was faced with far more temptation than his Old Kingdom ancestor. Human nature, however, does not change; it merely adapts to different circumstances. It would therefore be as grave a mistake to regard the Old Kingdom as an idyllic time of law and order as it would be to regard the New Kingdom as a time of desperate lawlessness.

Dynastic Egypt emerged as a literate state. While the question of which came first, writing or unification, remains a hotly debated academic point, it is clear that the employment of a nationwide system of writing played a major role in reinforcing the hierarchical social structure. From the very beginning, writing allowed the recording of ownership and the formalisation of hitherto flexible traditions. The development of an efficient civil service which could control the land and its people on behalf of the king soon followed. Effective land and water management, a function of the bureaucracy, was to prove crucial to the survival of the newly-formed country and, indeed, to the survival of the newly-created pharaoh.

The unification of Egypt had linked together a series of independent and not necessarily friendly city-states and petty chiefdoms to make one entity whose long, narrow geography made the imposition of central authority a difficult task. The kings of this new land were immediately faced with the problem of developing a national identity which would, as far as possible, ensure consistency of thought, belief, language and artistic convention. Included in this programme was the development of a national legal system, incorporating a law-code that would consolidate and clarify the various local rules and customs into one workable legal system. That the early kings were able to do this is self-evident. The idea of the judgement and punishment of the guilty by the king took deep root in official religion, and the last judgement of Osiris was to play an increasingly important role in the idiosyncratic development of Egyptian funerary tradition following the Old Kingdom.

Meanwhile peace and efficient land management brought prosperity. The new acceptance of a single ruler, and the channelling of all surplus resources towards that ruler, was soon to allow the building of the pyramids, an unprecedented expression of Pharaoh's ability to command his subjects. Pharaoh could not, however, rule Egypt single-handed. Throughout the Old and Middle Kingdoms much of his authority was delegated to the hereditary provincial governors, or nomarchs. The power of these local governors was to be severely weakened during the Twelfth Dynasty when Senwosret III eliminated much of the old feudal system, replacing it with a more professional and, it was hoped, more loyal bureaucracy staffed by the king's own appointees.

The written law-codes of Assyria, Babylonia, Hatti (the Hittite empire) and Israel have to a greater or lesser extent survived to add greatly to our understanding of these past societies. We know that Egypt, too, had an officially recognised system of rules and regulations, although we are less certain of the form in which these rules were maintained. Given the Egyptians' great respect for history and the historical precedent, plus their indefatigable habit of compiling lengthy administrative documents on every possible occasion, it would be amazing if these laws had not been committed to papyrus. The Greek historian Diodorus Siculus, writing during the first century BC, and deeply impressed by the efficient Egyptian legal system, tells us that these were indeed codified laws, written down and preserved in eight books or scrolls:

> The Egyptians showed great interest in the administration of justice ... for it was evident to them that if the offenders against the law were punished and the injured parties were afforded succour there would be an ideal correction of wrongdoing ... The entire body of the laws was written down in eight volumes which were placed before the judges.[2]

Diodorus, however, is not always the most reliable of witnesses and no trace of these eight books of law has yet been found.

As I write, our only tangible link with codified state law is a fragment of a demotic law book recovered from a broken jar discovered within a ruined building believed to be one of the temple archives of Hermopolis West (Tuna el-Gebel). This document, dated to the third century BC, deals with civil law – property leasing and inheritance rights.[3] Unfortunately, the books of legal cases maintained by the vizier's office for reference in future judgements have also been lost to us and so we have none of the statistics beloved of our modern politicians. We have no inkling of the crime and detection rates and no idea of how many convicts were executed, how many had their sentences commuted to a life of banishment in Pharaoh's work-gangs, how many were compelled to live minus ears and nose. Instead, our understanding of Egyptian law and order is taken from more indirect evidence: a random mixture of court documents, civil contracts, private writings, observed behaviour and fictional tales, plus a series of royal decrees that detail particular crimes and their specified punishments. Although the earliest of these royal decrees dates to the Old Kingdom, our information is heavily biased towards the New Kingdom, the time when Egypt's expanding empire required the services of ever-increasing numbers of middle-class bureaucrats to process an ever-increasing amount of documentation.

An unequal distribution of wealth and opportunity need not, of course, lead to crime. However, human nature being what it is, each social class was blessed with its fair share of miscreants and wrongdoers. The only limiting factor was access to resources, so that we find the poorer sections of the community restricted to the more simple and physical of offences, the petty crimes, thefts and murders. Meanwhile, members of the élite were able to exploit their exalted position and indulge in more cerebral, 'white-collar' crime, which might include bribery (both paid and received), corruption and fraud on a massive scale. Their wealth, of course, allowed them the additional luxury of paying others to commit crimes on their behalf.

The long record of dynastic offences ranges from the trivial and the antisocial – the villager accused of 'borrowing' his neighbour's donkey without permission – through burglary, robbery with violence, fraud, tax evasion, murder and, most heinous of all, regicide. Many of these are crimes with which we are all familiar today, although tomb-robbery, 'Egypt's second oldest profession', was a speciality developed as a direct response to specific Egyptian funerary beliefs. Bank robbery, in the absence of banks and, indeed, of money, was an impossibility; instead, gangs targeted the gigantic warehouses attached to the temples and palaces. Their spectacular ability to spirit away large quantities of material, apparently unseen and unheard, provides indirect confirmation that the bribery and corruption of officials was also a widespread phenomenon.

While punishment is usually obvious, 'crime' can sometimes be difficult to define. When considering the Egyptian evidence we may distinguish between entirely private offences which might be settled outside the court system, civil offences which might be resolved by private action through the court, and criminal offences – crimes against the king or the state which would certainly be prosecuted by the authorities. Occasionally these offences might overlap; a witness in a civil case might, for example, be found guilty of the crime of perjury or false litigation (time-wasting) and be punished accordingly. At all times, the state showed a marked reluctance to intervene in what it regarded as domestic affairs, and actions that today are frowned upon, such as casual domestic violence towards women, children, social inferiors or animals, would not necessarily attract the attention of the authorities. The state was generally reluctant to avenge the abused individual. Nevertheless, we do have a few rare examples of private offences being brought to the attention of the authorities and provoking them to take action to preserve public order.

The first category of offences, that of personal offences, is a wide-ranging one, stretching from mild social misdemeanours such as gluttony and drunkenness through immoral behaviour – the nobleman who failed to help the unprotected widow, the man who seduced married women – to offences against natural justice. All, however, were considered to be private matters and all might properly be resolved without recourse to the court. We have remarkably few accounts of crimes of violence, although the informal written records preserved at Deir el-Medina make it clear that aggressive behaviour was by no means unknown.

The surprising shortage of assaults, rapes, drunken brawls and fights over women may be the result of the differential preservation of evidence, with these offences being tried in a different, so-far undiscovered court. However, it is probably better explained by the fact that these, as private rather than state matters, were settled informally by the families or communities concerned. Parallels with more modern Egypt suggest that a simple murder, for example, is likely to have been resolved either by the payment of blood money or by the taking of a compensatory life. The community would assist in the delicate negotiations which would lead to a solution acceptable to both sides, and at Deir el-Medina it seems that the foremen had the authority to resolve such disputes before they escalated to a full feud.

Other matters, disputes over inheritance and property rights for example, needed to be settled in a formal manner. It was the right of any Egyptian man or woman to petition an official and to place a civil action before the local court, a tribunal made up of respected citizens which would be convened as and when needed. There was no jury and no professional lawyers; Diodorus tells us that the devious oratory of the lawyer would merely serve to confuse the issues (a sentiment that will strike a chord with many modern readers). Nor was there any official help in catching miscreants. The citizen was responsible for the presentation of his or her own case; he or she was required to provide the court with details of the dispute, witnesses and, of course, the defendant. This must have been a daunting responsibility for an ill-educated peasant:

> Custom dictated that the plaintiff should present in writing the details of his complaint; the charge, how the offence occurred; the injury or damage sustained. The defendant would then take the document and reply, again in writing, to each charge.[4]

Justice was, in theory, available to all regardless of sex, wealth or social status, although in practice a poor or insignificant claimant may have had some difficulty in proving a case against a social superior as the tendency was for the court to believe the wealthier petitioner. Prudence, as always, made sense: 'Do not go to court against your better when you have no protection against him,' advised the Late Period scribe Ankhsheshonq.[5] If women were summoned to appear before the local court less often than their menfolk, this would appear to be a reflection of the fact that they made fewer property transactions than men; where women do appear as plaintiffs they seem to have been well aware of their legal rights.

In the amusing and instructive Middle Kingdom *Tale of the Eloquent Peasant* we see civil justice in action, and learn how eloquence alone might help a man to win his case:

> Khun-Anup, a peasant farmer, was on his way to market, his donkeys laden with valuable produce. The way to the market led past the house and field of an unscrupulous, greedy man named Djehutinakht, employee of the High Steward Rensi. Djehutinakht saw the peasant and devised a cunning plan to steal both the donkeys and their loads. Rushing ahead of Khun-Anup he spread a sheet across the narrow road. He then forbad the peasant to step on either the sheet or the barley field which lay to the side of the road. As the other side of the road was bordered by the canal, Khun-Anup was forced to stand and argue the matter. As he did so one of his donkeys ate a morsel of barley. This is what Djehutinakht had been hoping for. He immediately asserted his right to compensation for the loss of the barley and, waving aside Khun-Anup's offer of reasonable payment, seized the donkeys. The two men quarrelled, Khun-Anup received a beating and Djehutinakht made off with his prize.
>
> Khun-Anup knew his rights and was not prepared to let

the matter drop. After a week spent pleading for the return of his property he appealed in person to Rensi. Rensi placed the matter before the magistrates who were at first inclined to disbelieve the unknown peasant. After hearing the loquacious Khun-Anup speak, however, they were amazed at his eloquence. Rensi, equally amazed, referred the matter to the king. The king was fascinated, he wanted to hear more. Poor Khun-Anup was forced to testify again and again before Rensi, with transcripts of his speeches being secretly passed to the king. Naturally this angered the peasant who turned against Rensi and received a severe beating for his pains. Eventually judgement was given. Khun-Anup won his case and received compensation for his loss while his persecutor lost all his property. Egyptian justice had triumphed once again![6]

More complex civil matters, and all criminal cases, would be investigated by government officials reporting directly to the permanent court of the vizier, deputy to the king. The court had the power to arrest, detain and question suspects, and was permitted to use torture as a means of verifying its witness statements. Crimes – that is, offences against the state – attracted the harshest of summary punishments. This is understandable. A crime was effectively a challenge to the authority of the king. Since the punishment served both as a warning to others and as a means of re-establishing the state's authority over the criminal, there was a danger that any show of leniency might be misinterpreted as weakness.

As in many societies where the life of the masses is held cheap, merely to be suspected of a crime was to invite physical abuse. Beatings were, for many, an accepted hazard of daily life. Schoolboys were flogged by their masters; servants were beaten by their overseers; the lower classes might be whipped by their superiors. Police officers went equipped with truncheons or leather batons to help their investigations, while the much-hated tax-collectors were armed with sticks which they were not slow to use.

The punishment of those whom the courts found guilty was both swift and brutal by modern Western standards, although not so by the standards of our relatively recent past. Prisons did exist, but imprisonment was both costly and non-productive, and was used only to hold those awaiting trial. Convicted criminals might be exiled to a work-gang or given a physical punishment ranging from beating and wounding through mutilation of the face to death by impaling on a post. Public executions never became the popular spectator events that they were in many societies, but they certainly did exist and the gruesome hieroglyphic symbol of a man pierced on a stake speaks for itself.

In the most serious cases punishment could, and often did, extend beyond the grave. From the very beginning of the dynastic age, Egyptian theology taught that for the spirit to enjoy any form of life after death the earthly body had to be preserved. The fate of the corpse was therefore a matter of paramount importance. Ideally, an Egyptian would die peacefully at home where friends and family could ensure that the correct embalming rituals were performed. Death abroad was to be avoided at all costs, while the loss of the corpse, as might occur in a case of drowning or burning, was a fate too horrible to contemplate. It therefore followed that any punishment that interfered with the preservation of the body was a very serious matter indeed. Lest this concern for the dead be seen as strange or irrational, it is perhaps worth remembering that, until relatively recently, the British state regularly inflicted punishment on the corpses of its executed criminals. Worse than a sentence of hanging was one of hanging followed by a trip to the medical school for dissection.

Dynastic history stretches over almost three thousand years from the unification of Upper and Lower Egypt in 3000 BC to the arrival of Alexander the Great in 332 BC. By convention this vast time-span is divided into a sequence of Kingdoms and Intermediate Periods, each of which is further subdivided into the Dynasties of associated rulers. Generally speaking, the Kingdoms were periods of strong central authority and effective rule, while the Intermediate Periods were times of civil unrest and near anarchy when a combination of internal and external factors (low Nile levels, famine, invaders) conspired to dislodge Pharaoh from his throne. It is telling that after, and even in some cases during, each of these disruptive periods the monarchy was restored along lines very similar to what had gone before.

Throughout the centuries the Egyptians maintained a love of stability, a suspicion of the unknown and an avoidance of needless experimentation. This reluctance to embark on change for change's sake resulted in the remarkable stability that characterises so many aspects of dynastic existence. While we should not fall into the trap of overestimating this stability – there were clearly many differences between life in the Old and New Kingdoms – it is impossible to think of any other society whose social structure, art, architecture, language and funerary practices demonstrate a comparable unbroken tradition. It is this continuity that makes possible a study such as this, incorporating the whole of dynastic Egypt.

# CHAPTER 1

## MAAT AND THE KING

At the very beginning of time existence was created. Out of the great sea of chaos emerged an island of order and tranquillity. At first only marsh plants thrived on this primordial mound but gradually, as time passed, divine and mortal life came into being. Eventually the land, her gods and her people flourished. Egypt – now the centre of the world – became a place of great beauty and abundance. With a glad heart the people set to work to till the fields and fish the river for the glory of their earthly king. Their king in turn devoted his life to serving the many deities who inhabited the pantheon and who protected the land and its people. Meanwhile, unseen and unheard, the waves of chaos continued to lap at the shores of existence, posing an invisible, ever-present threat to daily life.

Just as the world had been created, so it could be destroyed. Only the support of the gods could prevent Egypt from drowning in chaos. The survival of humankind was entirely dependent upon the goodwill of the deities, while the gods in turn depended upon the mortals for their daily offerings of food, drink and clothing. This interdependency kept the world in balance and ensured the preservation of Egypt. However, Egypt's deities were capricious beings, quick to take offence at perceived and actual slights. Their co-operation could never be taken for granted and it was essential that they were at all times treated with appropriate respect. Any deviation from officially sanctioned behaviour might provoke them to anger, particularly if that deviation involved the neglect of the official cults.

The *Tale of the Destruction of Mankind*, the Egyptian equivalent of the biblical story of Noah and the Mesopotamian legend of Gilgamesh, provided a horrible warning of what could happen if mortals ever grew rash enough to abandon the time-honoured traditions:

> The people of Egypt were plotting rebellion against their gods. Learning of this treachery, the great sun-god Re grew angry and determined to destroy all mankind. Re summoned his daughter Hathor, known as the Eye of Re, to carry out the slaughter. Hathor started her unsavoury work, and found that she enjoyed it. Re then relented of his impulse, but found that it was too late to stop Hathor. The god therefore devised a crafty plan. He instructed his priests to mix together red ochre and beer so that they looked like blood. The fields were flooded with this liquid and Hathor, seeing what she thought was blood, drank freely. She returned home to her father drunk, without completing her task. Thus mankind was saved.[1]

Egypt's long history confirmed that the gods were indeed capable of abandoning their people. The short-lived Amarna period, a time when the traditional gods were deliberately denied in favour of a single deity, was an experiment which few would choose to repeat. The lawless Intermediate Periods which separated the controlled Old, Middle and New Kingdoms provided further proof of the disasters that could beset a godless, kingless country, and caused the scribes to wail and lament:

> Behold, crime is everywhere ... the women are barren and
> none can conceive ... blood is everywhere ... The wealthy
> despair while the poor rejoice ... laughter has ceased and is
> no more, groaning and laments echo throughout the land
> ... the children of the nobles are dashed against the walls ...
> citizens are put to work at the grindstones ... noblemen go
> hungry and suffer.[2]

Chaos was by no means seen as an abstract concept or an empty
threat, and the untamed desert that bounded the fertile Nile Valley
served as a permanent reminder of the stark opposition of order
and disorder. Such marked physical contrasts were everywhere to
be seen. The fertile soil, the Black Land, contrasted with the barren
desert Red Land; the burning heat of the day contrasted with the
cool of the night; the living who inhabited the Nile Valley
contrasted with the dead who dwelt in the tombs and graves of the
desert.

The gods, then, would remain happy as long as Egypt
functioned properly. That is, as long as the people continued to
work for the benefit of the king while the king continued to work
for the benefit of the gods. This state of correct being, known to
the Egyptians as *maat*, was the opposite of chaos or *isfet*. There is
no single English word that we can use to translate *maat*, but the
concept is one that is relatively easy for us to understand. In its
widest form, *maat* was a condition of 'rightness'. As such, *maat*
may be understood to represent the status quo or stability,
although in certain contexts the term is translated more specifically as justice or truth.

Throughout the dynastic age, *maat* remained the most desirable
commodity in Egypt, eagerly sought after by both mortals and
gods. However, *maat* was a fragile, precarious thing that needed to
be protected by an intense conservatism and a strict adherence to
tradition. If everything was done correctly and as it always had
been there was a negligible chance of things going wrong. To

tamper with what had gone before, to institute change where none was needed, could pose a dangerous threat to *maat*. This belief that we can ensure success by replicating as far as possible the events leading to a previous success is a very human one. Even today, many of us develop our own private rituals for dealing with times of stress; the phenomenon of the examination candidate who 'knows' that the use of a particular pencil-case will substantially increase his or her chances of success is one that many readers will recognise.

The abstract concept of *maat* was personified in the goddess Maat, daughter of Re and representative of truth, justice and harmony. From the Old Kingdom onwards, Maat appears, often as the companion of the king, wearing a simple sheath dress with a single tall ostrich feather on her head. Maat was the counterpart of the mischievous and highly complex god Seth, who represented a controlled disruption and disorder and yet who had enough good qualities to ensure that he was respected and revered rather than shunned. Seth was allowed to take his place in the pantheon, and it was only at the very end of the dynastic age that he fell from his position of influence. Today, we tend to see Maat and Seth as elements in opposition, the direct equivalents of *maat* and *isfet*, just as one might envisage the opposing coexistence of God and Satan. This is, however, an oversimplification. To the ancient Egyptians, Maat and Seth appeared as the two complementary opposites – controlled order and controlled disorder – necessary to create a whole which was itself distinct from uncontrolled chaos.

If existence was consistently threatened by chaos, it was important that Egypt remain strong and unified in the face of danger. The maintenance of *maat* was the primary means of defence. Each individual could maintain his or her own *maat* by living a virtuous life; this involved honouring the gods, serving the king and respecting fellow mortals. Many upper-class males chose to highlight this aspect of their life in their so-called autobiographies, the short obituaries of self-praise that decorated the walls of their tombs:

> I have built this tomb from my rightful earnings without usurping any man's property . . . I am honoured by the king. I am honoured by the great god. I am a lover of goodness who hates wrongdoing.
>
> Extract from the tomb inscription of the Sixth Dynasty<br>provincial governor Inti

> I have come in peace at the completion of my life in the favour of the good god. I have done that which the people love, and that which pleases the gods. I have done as my king wished and have not ignored his commands. I have not wronged anyone. I have done right on earth.
>
> Extract from the prayer to Osiris in the Eighteenth Dynasty<br>Theban tomb of the vizier Ramose[3]

Of course, it would be naive to take these individuals at their own word. The autobiographies were formulae designed to appeal to the casual passer-by who might then be moved to make an offering to aid the deceased in the afterlife. As such, their presence serves as little more than confirmation that the tomb owner knew the correct way of decorating his tomb. The virtues listed are suspiciously vague and negative – 'I have done no wrong', 'I have not cheated the widow' – and we lack the specific, positive histories that might add credence to claims of a life of exemplary goodness. Nevertheless, the accepted morality of *maat* as illustrated in these texts was an important one for society as a whole. Not everyone did as they should, but the educated élite at least knew what they should be striving to do.

That society was capable of identifying good and bad actions is confirmed by the surviving didactic literature, a series of instruction texts, written from the Old Kingdom onwards, that tell the reader how he, for the reader is always assumed to be he, should behave. The advice given ranges from good table manners (the anonymous Old Kingdom author who addressed his instruction to Kagemni suggested that 'Gluttony is base, and should be reproved') to more important matters outlined by the New Kingdom scribe Amenemope:

> Guard against robbing a wretch or attacking a cripple . . .
> Pause before a foe, bend before an adversary . . . guard your
> tongue from harmful speech . . . do not covet the poor man's
> goods . . . do not cheat a man through writing . . . if you see
> someone who cheats, avoid him.[4]

This accepted recognition of right and wrong was particularly important as Egyptian theology, lacking a creed, teachings or, indeed, a system of belief, had little interest in promoting the moral or spiritual welfare of the people. Only the threat of divine judgement beyond death served to encourage good behaviour in life, and it was widely understood that it was possible for the devious to cheat this final court. State religion, the ancient equivalent of our modern science, had not developed to bring solace to the masses, but to provide explanations for aspects of life that would otherwise remain mysterious. Only one mortal, the king, was allowed to play the part of scientist in the religious laboratory.

The king, or Pharaoh, of Egypt was a unique individual. Born fully human, invariably the son of a mortal mother and in several instances the son of a non-royal father, he gained at his coronation an aura of divinity to become the one semi-divine being who stood part-way between the divine gods and the mortal Egyptians. At his death he would advance one further step to become fully divine. As he entered into his new state of semi-divine being the king to a certain extent lost his own individuality, becoming one with all the Pharaohs who had gone before and all who were to come. He was now the sole conduit through which the gods communicated with mankind, and vice versa. His existence was vital to both heaven and earth. Only the king could make the offerings that pleased the gods; only the king could ensure that the people complied with the wishes of the gods. Pharaoh was therefore essential to the wellbeing of Egypt and, as history showed, any king – an infant, a foreigner, even a woman – was better than none. The absence of a king would invariably be seen as an offence against *maat*.

The duties of the king were at once simple and awesome. To him fell the responsibility of maintaining cosmic order. He, and he alone, was charged with 'judging humanity and propitiating the gods, and setting order [*maat*] in the place of disorder'.[5] Many kings highlighted this aspect of their role by publishing 'restoration texts': texts that claim that the new monarch has once again brought order to an uncomfortably disordered land. Tutankhamen, for example, tells us of the chaos that preceded his accession:

> When his majesty arose as king the temples of the gods and goddesses, from Elephantine to the Delta, had fallen into decay, their shrines had collapsed in desolation and had become ruins overrun with weeds ... The land was topsy-turvy and the gods had turned their back on Egypt.[6]

Naturally, Tutankhamen set to work to restore the gods to their former exalted position and Egypt once again flourished under his rule.

While Tutankhamen's claim to be a restorer of *maat* was rooted in fact, kings who enjoyed peaceful reigns were forced to borrow the chaos of earlier times. In a clear reference to the Second Intermediate Period, for example, the female Pharaoh Hatchepsut claimed to have 'raised up what was dismembered, even from the first time when the Asiatics were in Avaris of the North Land, with roving hordes in the middle of them overthrowing what had been made'.[7] That the Hyksos had in fact been expelled from Avaris many years before her birth did not matter. Hatchepsut as monarch was fully justified in claiming the achievements of her predecessors as her own. Other monarchs contented themselves with smaller-scale deeds. The clearing of the sand from the Sphinx was a popular restoration, while the mighty Ramesses II started his reign by bringing order to his father's neglected temple at Abydos.

It was logical that the king, as upholder of *maat*, should take sole responsibility for the maintenance of law and order amongst his people. In modern terms this was both a civil and a religious duty, although the Egyptians themselves would have been unlikely to draw such a distinction. As the head of the civil service the monarch was naturally head of the judiciary; he was the supreme judge and the ultimate court of appeal. He upheld the laws and punished the guilty in order to ensure the safety and stability of his country. At the same time, the king was the chief priest of all cults. Any offence against law and order could be viewed as a religious matter, as an offence against *maat*. Such a violation needed to be avenged for the safety of Egypt. Punishment of the guilty therefore served a threefold purpose: it reasserted the power of the king, served as a warning to others, and, it was hoped, pleased the gods by providing obvious proof of the restoration of *maat*.

The image of Pharaoh as the personal messenger of justice to the enemies of the state is one that persisted throughout the dynastic age. The crook and flail of Osiris, adopted by the king, served to symbolise the principal royal duties of leadership and punishment. More obviously the ubiquitous 'smiting scene', a set-piece image depicting the king wielding a club, scimitar or sword to kill the foe who cringes at his feet, encapsulated the essence of Egyptian kingship for over three thousand years.[8]

The earliest of these scenes is found on the 'Narmer palette' (now displayed in Cairo Museum) where the probable unifier of Egypt is about to despatch a token enemy. Narmer stands tall and proud in his white crown, his club raised in his right hand. The defeated enemy recognises the superiority of the Egyptian king and, making no attempt to struggle, appears resigned to his fate. On the reverse of the palette is Narmer in the form of a bull goring an enemy. In a more ancient variation on the same animal theme, the unidentified local ruler of the pre-dynastic 'Battlefield palette' (now in pieces, two of which are housed in the Ashmolean Museum, Oxford, and the British Museum, London) appears as a lion to maul a hapless foreigner.

It is generally assumed that the smiting scene represents the symbolic sacrifice of the defeated foreigner before the victorious gods of Egypt. But, given the happy acceptance of animal sacrifice throughout the dynastic age plus the contempt felt for all prisoners of war, it may be that such scenes should more properly be read as a literal representation of an occasional ritual act. Murder was forbidden – it was an offence against *maat* – yet the king was allowed to inflict the death penalty on his own people. The killing of a foreigner, the living representative of Egypt's enemies, may therefore not have been taboo.

There is, however, little further evidence for the practice of regally-sanctioned human sacrifice in dynastic Egypt.[9] No contemporary documents detail such killings and Herodotus, for one, denies its existence. Diodorus Siculus begs to differ:

> Red oxen may be sacrificed because it is believed that red was the colour of Typhon [Seth] who plotted against Osiris and whom Isis punished for the murder of her husband. Men also of Typhon's colour, in the earliest days might be sacrificed by the kings at the tomb of Osiris. Now, few Egyptians are red, although most foreigners are and this is why the story spread amongst the Greeks.[10]

Manetho, recorded by Plutarch, refines this account, adding the means of execution: 'they burned living men . . . and winnowing the ashes they scattered them abroad.'[11] Even more remote is the traditional story of how Busiris, king of Egypt, attempted to sacrifice Hercules at Memphis, a legend that Herodotus emphatically dismisses as a 'silly tale'. It seems that Egypt, with her mysterious animal-headed deities and her curious funerary practices, stimulated the imagination of the classical writers, who were prepared to believe that almost anything was possible in the land of the Nile:

> We could see the great numbers of robbers, fully armed. They had made an altar of mud and placed a coffin near it. Then two of them brought forward a girl, her arms tied behind her back . . . First they poured libations over her then they led her round the coffin . . . one of the acolytes laid her down on her back and tied her to pegs fixed in the ground . . . then taking a sword he plunged it into the heart, dragging it downwards into her belly to release the entrails. Her bowels gushed forth into their hands and they placed them on the altar. When they were cooked the band cut them into pieces, shared them out and ate them.[12]

Archaeological evidence for human sacrifice is scanty to the point of non-existence. Perhaps the most convincing artefact that can be cited in this context is a curious wooden, frame-like structure recovered in 1960 from the south side of the Great Pyramid of King Khufu at Giza. After comparison with a stone block recovered from Karnak, which bears the image of a prisoner displayed on a ship in a wooden cage, the Giza object has (very) tentatively been identified by some experts as a cage used to house prisoners prior to ritual execution. On the basis that the most mundane explanation is more often than not the true one, however, it would be equally valid to argue that the object represents a gigantic packing case used to protect masonry or statuary being transported around the Giza plateau.[13]

If the actual execution of an enemy was forbidden, perhaps magic could be employed to achieve the same ends? The Egyptians certainly thought so. Throughout the dynastic age we have evidence for the use of substitutes – wax figures, pottery and wooden statuettes, inscribed bowls and plates – which would be named and then 'killed' in a voodoo-like smashing or melting ritual. This symbolic killing in absentia was used both by individuals and by the state, which found it a useful means of dealing with enemies living beyond the physical reach of the Egyptian army:

> All rebels in this land, all people, all officials, all subjects, all males, all females, all eunuchs, all women, all leaders, all Nubians, all soldiers, all messengers, all allies and all confederates of all foreign lands who might rebel ... who may plot, who may fight, who may talk of fighting, or who may talk of rebelling against Upper and Lower Egypt will be destroyed for all time.[14]

Pharaoh was the ultimate law enforcer. In an ideal world he could perhaps rely upon the goodwill of his people who, striving to maintain their own personal *maat*, would need few if any laws. In practice, it was found necessary to lay down rules of conduct, some of which were given the force of law, others of which remained as customs. The books of Egyptian law mentioned by Diodorus Siculus, if they ever existed in concrete form, are now lost to us and we are forced to guess that they included the basic rules necessary to preserve the person and property of the king and his gods.

Fortunately for the modern historian, individual monarchs from time to time supplemented the state laws with personal decrees detailing one or a series of particular offences and their punishment. These 'exemption decrees' were carved in stone for all to see, and several have survived the ravages of time. The earliest known example dates to the Fifth Dynasty, when King Neferirkare exempted the Abydos temple from taxation and issued a stern warning to those who might be tempted to ignore his command:

> If any man of the district shall take any royal mortuary priests who are on a field of the god ... He shall be sent to the granite quarry and his harvest share of barley and emmer shall be given to ...
>
> Any magistrate, person attached to the royal property, or possessor of a royal income who does wrong according to that which my majesty has commanded, shall be surrendered to the court. His land, people and possessions shall be taken.[15]

A similar exemption decree, issued by Pepi II for the temple of Min at Koptos, came with the injunction that any offending official 'shall be taken to the Hall of Horus ... my majesty does not allow that they be pure in the pyramid.' The punishment, then, for ignoring the word of the king, would extend beyond the grave with the guilty party denied burial in the royal necropolis – a serious matter for those who believed that proximity to the king in death would be highly beneficial in the afterlife. To be granted a place in the royal necropolis was to be guaranteed a decent, well-guarded tomb where the deceased had a reasonable chance of lying undisturbed for all eternity.

Later, the exemption decree issued by the First Intermediate Period king Demedjibtawy, intended to protect the mortuary statues and endowment of his official Idy, indicated that not only those who performed the misdeed, but also any who knew of it and failed to report it, would be punished:

Moreover, with regard to any royal representative or magistrate who does not confiscate the property of any man who does such things . . . he will be stripped of his office, and will have no legal claim to his property. Nor will his children have any legal claim to it. The magistrate who punishes these things, however, will remain in office.[16]

Demedjibtawy's stark statement, 'My Majesty cannot allow . . . that they will be among the living,' is open to interpretation: is he threatening that the offender will lose his life, or merely his liberty?

The best preserved of these exemption decrees is that issued by the Nineteenth Dynasty monarch Seti I to protect the Nubian estate that he had given to his cenotaph temple at Abydos, intending that all the income from the estate should go directly to the temple. Seti carved his decree high in the cliff face at Nauri, in Nubia, where it served as a stark warning to those who might be tempted to steal from the gods:

> His Majesty has commanded that ordinance be made for the House of Millions of Years of Menmaatre 'The Heart is at Ease in Abydos' on water and on land throughout the provinces of Upper and Lower Egypt: to prevent interference with any person belonging to the House in the whole land, whether man or woman; to prevent interference with any goods belonging to this estate in the whole land; to prevent the taking of any people belonging to this estate by capture from one district for another district . . .
>
> As to any Viceroy of Kush, any foreign chief, any mayor, any inspector or any person who shall take any person belonging to the House . . . punishment shall be done to him by beating him with two hundred blows and five open wounds, together with exacting the work of the person belonging to the Residence from him for every day that he shall spend with him, to be given to the House . . .

Now as to any high officer, any superintendent of the land belonging to this estate, any keeper of plough-oxen, any inspector who shall interfere with the boundary of lands belonging to the House ... punishment shall be done to him by the cutting off of his ears, he being put to be a cultivator in the Residence ...

As to any keeper of cattle, any keeper of hounds, any herdsman ... who shall give any head of animals belonging to the House by defalcation to another ... punishment shall be done to him by casting him down and impaling him on a stake, forfeiting his wife and children and all his property to the House and extracting the herd of animals from him to whom he shall have given it at the rate of a hundred to one.[17]

Seti's decree hints at a lack of cohesion between various government departments, with rival revenue-collecting officers squabbling over the right to tax the same piece of land. It seems that the divine assets needed to be protected as much, if not more, from the grasping hands of the tax-collectors, harem officials, local mayors and inspectors as from the common criminal.

We can see that the official punishment for ignoring the king's exemptions has evolved, by the New Kingdom, from the confiscation of property and the loss of burial rights to physical chastisement, with the precise number of blows and wounds specified. All the crimes detailed in Seti's decree may be classed as thefts from the god, but some are understood to be more serious than others. To borrow a worker on a temporary basis is a relatively minor crime; to move the field boundaries is more serious. Most serious of all, presumably because it involves a breach of official duty, is the stealing of the god's cattle by the very herdsmen employed to protect them; in this case the punishment is death by impaling.

A marginally less bloodthirsty inscription was carved on the temple wall at Wadi Mia (Kanais). Here Seti had dug a well to provide water for the quarrying expeditions who were frequent visitors to the eastern desert. Again, his aim was to protect the supply of gold that was destined for the Abydos temple treasury:

> I have appointed a band of gold washers. I appointed them as a new band in order that they should remain for me. I did not take them from any other band . . . But as to any official who shall suggest to his lord that he remove my workmen and put them to a different task, he is destined for the fire that will burn his body, for the flames that shall eat his limbs.[18]

This appears to be a curse rather than a specific statement of law, contrasting the blessings that are to be heaped on those who heed Seti's word with the fate that awaits those who do not. It seems that the offender is destined to enjoy the flames of hell rather than to be burned alive.

Some thirty years earlier Horemheb, the first strong king to rule Egypt after the Amarna Period, had found himself faced with a demoralised country on the verge of civil disintegration. Over a quarter of a century of weak rule had allowed the state administration to grow lazy and complacent, and now bribery and corruption infested every tier of the bureaucracy, making efficient government almost impossible. The new king started as he meant to go on. In a symbolic tidying-up operation, reminiscent of the 'restoration works' of earlier monarchs, he issued a decree outlining a programme of reforms designed to streamline the legal and administrative systems and overhaul the palace administration. Although this text is not well preserved, the specific penalties for those who might disobey the king's law have been preserved in three instances:

> If there is a man who wants to pay his taxes . . . and there is anyone who interferes and takes away his craft the law shall

be applied against him in the form of the cutting off of his nose, he being sent to Sile ...

If there is any man who interferes with those who ... and those who supply the harem and the offerings of the gods ... the law shall be applied against him in the form of the cutting off of his nose, he being sent to Sile ...

But as for any soldier about whom it shall be said, 'he goes about and takes hides away,' starting from today the law shall be applied against him by inflicting upon him one hundred blows and five open wounds, and taking from him the hide which has been unlawfully acquired.

Corruption, too, was to be treated as a serious offence:

But as for any official concerning whom one shall hear, 'he sits to administer justice in the court which has been set up for administering justice, and yet he violates justice therein,' it shall be considered to be a great capital crime.[19]

The decree, while appearing to protect the common man from the official or soldier who might be tempted to abuse his authority, was once again designed to protect those assets that should properly be paid to the state or to the temple. By the use of clever wording, Horemheb was able to appear as the champion of the underclasses while acting to preserve his own interests.

Despite his personal responsibility for the maintenance of law and order, time would not permit the king to involve himself in all court cases. He was forced to appoint deputies who would hear cases on his behalf, presiding himself over only the most important of trials and urgent of appeals, and rubber-stamping the death penalties imposed by his courts. The immediate deputy to the king was the vizier who would either in person, or through his office, deal with routine criminal and the more important civil matters. However, when theft on a massive scale was discovered in

Thebes during the reign of Ramesses II, the king appointed his son and heir, Crown Prince Ramesses, as judge, a clear indication of the severity of the offence. We are fortunate in having a lengthy transcript of this case preserved on an ostracon, although the names of the principal players are now lost.

The story is as follows.[20] A government official with responsibility for the warehouses attached to some of the Theban temples had started to transfer the gods' goods first to his father's house and thence to his own private store. No one noticed as vast amounts of property started to disappear. Eventually, the thief was transferred to another government post, that of inspector of cattle in the northern Delta region. Prestigious as the new appointment was, it left little scope for fraud, and so while the man moved north to start his new career, his wife and daughter remained in Thebes to carry on stealing from the warehouses. Eventually, however, the pitcher went to the well once too often, and a scribe named Hatiay noticed that the lady was entering the warehouses without authority. A complaint was filed and the lady was taken in for questioning over the disappearance of, amongst other things, large quantities of wine, linen, leather sandals and salt, 20,000 bushels of grain, livestock including 30 bulls, and even several chariots!

> She was taken to the Great Law-court to appear before the Hereditary Prince and the chief officials. She was asked, 'Why do you open two storerooms of the royal domain without the controller's knowledge?' She replied, 'These were places which my husband used to control.' The judge then said to her, 'Yes, your husband did have the duty of administering the domain, but he was removed from that post and appointed to another office.'

The scale of the goods listed as stolen hints at the immense wealth hidden within the storehouses and tombs of Thebes. No wonder the locals – those who knew of these hidden riches – were tempted! Now the husband was summoned to appear before the court and asked to account for the actions of his women. However, far from confessing to his misdeeds, he launched a spirited counterattack on the king's officers. On oath he declared, 'If anything is found in my father's possession I will repay it double. The caretakers of the king's estate took the property, each and every one of them.' In fact, he swore, the king's officers had treated him so badly that he was about to bring a case against them! Unfortunately, the end of the case is lost and we will never know the fate of the man, his wife and his daughter. As theft from the Theban temples was a criminal offence attacking both the gods and the state, the penalty for such rampant greed may well have been death.

# CHAPTER 2

# THE VIZIER:
# UPHOLDER OF JUSTICE

User, vizier or *tjaty* to the Eighteenth Dynasty king Tuthmosis III, employed the scribe Amenemhet as a steward. Amenemhet, proud of his links with Egypt's greatest official, has left us an admirably clear summary of his master's achievements:

> The scribe Amenemhet, justified, says:
>
> User, mayor of Thebes and vizier, did what the king loves: he raised up *maat* to its lord ... reporting daily on all his effective actions.
>
> User, mayor of Thebes and vizier, did what the gods love: he enforced the laws and laid down rules, administered the temples, provided the offerings, allotted the food and offered the beloved *maat*.
>
> User, mayor of Thebes and vizier, did what the nobility and the people love: he protected both rich and poor, provided for the widow without a family and pleased the revered and the old.[1]

Here we see the three duties of the vizier clearly defined; he serves the king, the gods and the people. The viziers themselves were not content with such a brief job-description. User's successor Rekhmire, vizier to Tuthmosis III and Amenhotep II, provides us with a lengthy, illustrated explanation of his official role. The extravagant text that he ordered carved on his tomb wall, today known as the *Duties of the Vizier*, was not original. Versions of the same text have been recognised in the tombs of User (TT 131), Amenemope (TT 29, Eighteenth Dynasty) and Paser (TT 106, Nineteenth Dynasty) and it seems likely that all four viziers were making use of a much earlier work, possibly one composed during the late Middle Kingdom. A brief extract from *The Duties* is sufficient to demonstrate the wide ranging responsibilities of the New Kingdom vizier:[2]

> The sealing of the strongrooms at the correct hour and their opening at the correct hour shall be reported to him ... the condition of the southern and northern guard posts shall be reported to him ... Everyone leaving and entering the palace shall be reported to him ... the overseers of the policemen, the policemen and the district overseers shall report to him ...
>
> If a serious accusation is brought against one of the workers in his office he ... shall be taken to the judgement hall. It is the vizier who should punish his wrongdoing according to the offence ... If anyone is not efficient in carrying out his duty the vizier shall question him and if the vizier is convinced of the man's guilt his name shall be entered in the criminal register which is kept in the great prison.
>
> It is he who appoints the head magistrates ... they will report to him the matters accomplished under their jurisdiction ... He shall arrange the mobilisation of the troops who escort the king as he travels up and down stream ... It is he who despatches men to cut down sycamore trees ... He who sends regional officers to construct dykes throughout the whole land ... Every plea should be reported to him.

Unfortunately we have no Old or Middle Kingdom text to

parallel *The Duties* and so, although we know that the office existed as early as the Second Dynasty and may well have developed even earlier, our knowledge of the pre-New Kingdom vizier's role is somewhat constrained. We do, however, know that the earliest viziers were close relatives of the king, a custom that continued until the Twelfth Dynasty when the administrative reorganisation of Senwosret III, intended to reduce the hereditary power of local rulers, actually strengthened the power of the vizier by decreasing the power of the provincial rulers.

Throughout the Second Intermediate Period the vizierate, now very much a hereditary position, remained the constant force in Egyptian administration while a succession of ephemeral kings came and went. With the imposition of political unity at the start of the New Kingdom, the monarchy regained much of its former strength. The vizierate, managing to retain some of the power gained during the Middle Kingdom, was no longer hereditary, although certain eminent political families produced successive viziers. New kings did not automatically appoint a new vizier on their succession and so, much as the modern British civil service continues as governments come and go, the 'reigns' of the viziers and the reigns of the kings overlapped to provide a seamless succession of central authority which facilitated the smooth running of the country.

During the Eighteenth Dynasty Egypt's rapidly expanding wealth caused a huge increase in internal administration. The office of vizier was now split in two, a prudent measure designed to ease the workload while ensuring that no one bureaucrat could grow powerful enough to challenge the authority of Pharaoh. From this time onwards, there would be a northern or Memphite vizier who controlled both Lower Egypt and the Delta region, and a southern or Theban vizier whose duties included responsibility for the royal necropolis and the associated workmen's village of Deir el-Medina. Unfortunately, records of the activities of the northern viziers, possibly the more influential of the pair, have been largely lost, and most of our information concerns the southern viziers. These included Rekhmire, User, Amenemope and Paser amongst their number.

Effectively, the New Kingdom vizier combined the roles of deputy and personal assistant to the king. In consequence, his official presence was that of a semi-royal being tinged with a hint of the divine. The vizier represented law and order. Seated on an imposing throne, his regalia spread out before him, he was an awesome being. Supplicants introduced to his chamber were expected to bow low as if in the presence of royalty; indeed, a court official would forcibly bend the unfortunate supplicant into the correct ignominious position. Prominently displayed amongst the vizier's paraphernalia, as shown in the tomb of Rekhmire, were forty curious leather-bound objects. Historians once believed these to be the lost books of Egyptian law written on leather scrolls, but today it is generally accepted that they were ceremonial rods or whips, the symbols of the vizier's authority.

The vizier's theoretical responsibility, like that of the king, was the maintenance of *maat*. In practical terms, his duties were all internal and administrative, with foreign affairs, control of the army and control of the priesthood largely left to others. The vizier managed the country on behalf of the king: he headed the civil service, including the judiciary and the prisons, managed the royal palace, supervised the management of the agricultural land and was even occasionally required to act as a stand-in for the monarch.

The vizier himself, of course, had to be a man of impeccable conduct, impervious to the bribery and corruption that posed an ever-present threat to the efficiency of the bureaucracy. The sage Amenemope deplored all forms of official corruption, making his views known to the Ramesside reader:

Do not bring down the men of the magistrates' court in order to brush aside the righteous man. Do not pay too much attention to him who is clothed in gleaming garments; instead have regard for him who is shabbily dressed. Do not accept the reward of the powerful man and then persecute the weak for him ... Do not equip yourself with false documents ... Do not falsify the oracle in the scrolls and thus tamper with the will of the gods.[3]

But how did anyone choose a trustworthy servant, one who would be impervious to bribes? To the New Kingdom author of the *Instruction for Merikare* the answer was clear – he must chose a wealthy man:

Promote your officials so that they may enforce your laws. One who is already wealthy at home will not be biased, for being rich he has no need. The poor man does not speak truly, and one who says 'I wish that I had ... ' is not straightforward; he is biased towards the one who can provide a reward. Great indeed is that great man whose own men are great.[4]

On the wall of his tomb Rekhmire, a suitably wealthy man, tells us how he himself acted with utmost propriety at all times: 'I was the heart of my Lord [Tuthmosis III], the ears and eyes of the sovereign ... I raised *maat* up to heaven ... I never took a bribe from anyone.' Well, he would say that, wouldn't he? No official was going to confess to anything less than perfect behaviour in his tomb. In fact, we know that Rekhmire's glittering career came to an unexpectedly abrupt end. The details of his loss of office have not been preserved but there is a strong possibility that he was involved in some form of scandal or abuse of power.

As the *Instructions for Merikare* recognised, temptation for the vizier took the form of bribery. Thus we find the Nineteenth Dynasty vizier Preemheb accepting a gift of five servants shortly before promoting the clearly unsuitable Paneb to the position of

Deir el-Medina foreman; and the Twentieth Dynasty Khaemwaset, vizier at the time of the great Theban tomb-robberies, working in league with the corrupt mayor Paweraa. We shall meet these unsavoury characters again in Chapter 9. More minor breaches of propriety involved the Deir el-Medina villagers giving 'presents' or 'baksheesh' to the vizier in order to speed the payment of their overdue rations. On one occasion during the reign of Ramesses IX two beds were sent to Thebes, while during the time of Ramesses X two chests and a writing-set followed the same route. That the vizier was able to exploit the villagers as labourers was obvious to all; his ability to divert the workforce to his own projects was accepted as a perk of his position.

Faced with his wide range of duties the vizier, like the king, was forced to delegate. He was assisted in his work by an office of scribes, not mere clerks but highly respected civil servants empowered to act as agents of the vizier himself. The vizier's messengers, his means of communicating with his far-flung subordinates, were entitled to be treated with the respect due to the vizier's ambassador. Anyone forcing a messenger to bow low might be punished 'with any type of repression in addition to the amputation of a limb'. The vizier's scribes were used to filter out the more mundane work, the day-to-day running of the central administration, including the judiciary, leaving the vizier free to concentrate on the more complex and important matters.

Because the vizier's authority extended outside the confines of the central bureaucracy to include the correct management of the land and its people, we find him involved in the appointment of all key figures of local government, who then acted as his remote agents. Thus he was able to exert his control over the provinces with a hand-picked and presumably loyal band of local mayors, district councillors and magistrates, all directly answerable to his office. The vizier had the power to summon and if necessary judge and punish these local leaders, a power that he did not hesitate to use. A scene in the Old Kingdom tomb of the vizier Khentika shows five such local dignitaries, three of whom are grovelling before their lord while two are forced by servants to bend low. Behind them are two further unfortunates who, having been found guilty of an unspecified misdemeanour, have been tied to a post to be beaten with a stick.

The security of the royal palace was considered a matter of major importance, with everything and everyone passing through the palace gates subjected to close scrutiny. Whether these measures were intended to protect the king, his property, or both, is not clear; Egyptian history tends to shy away from any suggestion that the king could ever have become a victim of his people. We do know that the vizier assumed personal responsibility for the guarding of the palace gates and for the appointment of the palace police, and that both the chief of the palace police and the palace manager reported directly to him. Any breaches of discipline by the palace staff were also dealt with by the vizier. This responsibility for court security applied even when the king and his court were touring the country. As the dynastic kings, well aware of the dangers of becoming isolated in their capital city, tended to spend much of their time travelling up and down the Nile, this must have provided the vizier with a constant logistical headache.

As the head of state bureaucracy, the vizier had ultimate judicial control over the civil service, with responsibility both for internal matters and for matters relating to the general public. No mere supervisor had the authority to judge a subordinate's work; all complaints had to be reported to the vizier and he alone could investigate breaches of civil service rules, be they accidental or deliberate, civil or criminal. He, too, was the sole arbitrator when a member of the public petitioned against an inequitable ruling. The vizier decided upon the punishment, usually loss of office and the associated endowment, for those found guilty of bad or careless work. When appropriate, the vizier could decree that the name of the offender be entered upon the register held in the forbidding-sounding 'Great Prison' of Thebes. This register was available for consultation should the subsequent conduct of an employee be called into question.

The 'Great Prison', one of a series of prisons and small local jails dotted about Egypt, was an institution with several functions, which came directly under the control of the vizier's office. As the repository of the criminal records, the prison served as the legal archive, employing a suitably large staff of scribes to ensure that the files were kept up to date. Within the precincts of the prison was a law-court; here a tribunal could be convened to hear criminal and complex civil cases. Those found guilty could be transferred immediately to the prison cells where they would languish for the brief period between sentencing and punishment. Criminal trials were often short, and punishment, carried out within the prison, followed hot on the heels of a guilty verdict.

Finally, the prison served as a barrack or workhouse for those who had been conscripted by the local authority, acting on the order of the vizier in his role as manager of the land, under the system of corvée, or temporary forced labour:

> The field-worker cries out more than the guinea-fowl. His voice is louder than that of a raven. His fingers have grown sore with an excess of stench. When he is taken away to be enrolled in Delta labour he is in tatters. He suffers when he goes to the island, and sickness is his reward. The forced labour is then tripled. When he returns home from the marshes he is worn out, for the corvée has wrecked him.[5]

The professional architects, engineers, artisans and labourers engaged on the national construction sites were all in the employ, either full-time or part-time, of the state. However, it was sometimes found necessary to supplement their numbers with unskilled, conscripted labour borrowed from the local towns, villages and hamlets. The workers so assembled were divided into work-gangs and compelled to toil for a specified length of time, with board, lodging, clothing and medical services provided by the state, on a project such as the building of a pyramid, the repairing of a dyke or the excavation of a canal.

While of undoubted benefit to the community as a whole, the individual conscripts received no personal reward for their hard work; indeed, having been snatched from their daily routines, they were often considerably disadvantaged. Even less fortunate were those taken from the fields to serve as reluctant soldiers in the Old and Middle Kingdom armies:

> When His Majesty [Pepi I] took action against the Asiatic sand-dwellers, His Majesty made an army of many tens of thousands from all of Upper Egypt: from Yebu in the south to Medenyt in the north; from Lower Egypt; from all of the Delta and from Sedjer and Khen-Sedjru.[6]

Naturally the corvée was universally hated, so much so that it proved necessary to 'persuade' the people to perform their civic duty by making it illegal to shirk the call-up.

Only a favoured few were automatically exempt from this service, their status protected by statute. The penalty for ignoring a corvée exemption could be severe. During the Old Kingdom Pepi II classed it as a criminal matter. In the New Kingdom decree quoted in Chapter 1, Seti I specified a punishment of two hundred lashes, five open wounds and a replacement of the work-days lost for anyone illegally diverting the exempt workforce. When the Nineteenth Dynasty Memphite official Bakenptah was caught in the act of diverting eight corvée workers from officially sanctioned work at the Temple of Thoth to unauthorised stone-dragging at the nearby Temple of Hauron, his nemesis Djehutiemheb took a dim view of the situation, writing to him: 'You should let them go at once ... Death is how I am involved with you.'[7]

The wealthy, however, had little cause to worry about the call-up. If they could not wangle an official exemption, the provision of a substitute worker, or the application of a suitable bribe, would cause the scribes to look the other way. The officials responsible for making the final selection of the workforce were in a position of great power. They could select and reject at will, and it would appear that abuses of the system were rife.

Once enlisted, there could be no escape. Papyrus Brooklyn 35.1446, a Twelfth Dynasty document originally recovered in hundreds of fragments and painstakingly pieced together by the staff of Brooklyn Museum, lists the names of some seventy-five men and one woman who were misguided enough to flee the prison compound without completing their designated work.[8] The penalty for such antisocial behaviour was well-known, and the vizier's office did not hesitate to issue the necessary warrants: 'An order was issued to the Great Prison ... to release his [or her] people from the law-court and to execute against him [or her] the law relating to one who deliberately absconds for six months.'

As soon as it had been discovered that the labourers had vanished, their families had been taken hostage and either transported to Thebes or confined to their own homes. This, in a society lacking money and whose poorer members had few seizable assets, was the logical method of exerting pressure on the fugitives to return. The same treatment seems to have been extended to the families of army deserters: 'Be he at large, or be he detained, the soldier suffers. If he runs and joins the deserters all his people are imprisoned.'[9]

Now, perhaps because the corvée deserter had been recaptured, the families were to be set free and the offender alone left to face the consequences of his or her actions. Not all the hostage families were automatically released, however, and one unfortunate peasant, Montuhotep son of Sabes, received an unusually tough sentence which was extended to his close relations: 'An order was issued to the Great Prison for his being given to the plough-lands together with his people, for ever.'

In citing specific punishments for a series of well-defined crimes, the Brooklyn papyrus comes close to confirming what we have already suspected: that Egypt did indeed have a codified law. Here, subtle differences are recognised between the various types of desertion. There are individual penalties for 'those who desert', 'one who deliberately deserts for six months', 'the deliberate desertion of one's labours', 'fleeing without performing his task' and 'one who flees the prison'. Deliberate, or planned, desertion appears to be the most serious offence, while the length of absence is also to be taken into account when punishing the fugitive.

We have seen that the vizier took responsibility for justice within the civil service and that he, via his office, punished those found guilty of evading the corvée. That he was also expected to receive petitions and act as judge in wider-ranging matters concerning the general public is made clear in the *Installation of the Vizier*, also inscribed in the tomb of Rekhmire. Here the king speaks to his new vizier:

> Behold, the petitioner of Upper and of Lower Egypt comes to receive judgement in the hall of the vizier. Then you shall see that everything is done as specified by the law, that everything is done in a precise manner in letting a man plead his innocence ... A magistrate should act according to the rules and do what is specified ... Do not make an improper judgement; biased behaviour is abhorrent to the god ... Do not dismiss a petitioner before you have heard his words ... The court in which you sit contains a hall with a record of all judgements ... Do not act as you wish in matters where the law is known.[10]

The vizier, then, was to act as an impartial judge in accordance with the established traditions of Egyptian justice. Each petitioner, plaintiff or defendant was to be treated equally, regardless of social status, and each case was to be considered on its own merit. Justice was to be available to all, and the duty of care which the élite and those in authority owed to the poor and insignificant was not to be abandoned at the court door. Legal precedent, or case-law, was considered very important, and the vizier was expected to consult the 'record of all judgement' preserved in his office as and when necessary.

The majority of cases brought before the vizier were complex civil matters, often long-running disputes over land or property rights which the local courts were unable to handle and where the establishment of a legal precedent was an important consideration. Criminal trials, the judging and sentencing of those found guilty of offences against the state, tended to be simple cases bereft of legal technicalities and involving a prescribed punishment. Here, however, the vizier's office would have the responsibility for investigating the reported crime, summoning the witnesses and considering their statements before pronouncing judgement. Some minor crimes, small-scale tax evasion for example, might never reach the great court; tax defaulters tended to attract summary punishment from the dreaded tax-collector.

Perhaps the lengthiest and most complicated lawsuit ever to involve the vizier was one that was finally settled during the reign of Ramesses II.[11] The case had originated almost three hundred years before, in the time when King Ahmose rewarded his loyal followers by granting them land. One such follower, Neshi, was given an estate near Memphis. This estate remained undivided in the family for many generations, managed by a single trustee who divided the profits between all those entitled to a share. Unfortunately, during the reign of Horemheb, the family started to feud. An application was made to the law-court for the land to be divided, and it was eventually decided that the lady Wernuro should manage the land on behalf of her siblings. Not everyone was happy with this decision. Her sister Takhuru raised a legal challenge to the judgement, requesting that the estate be split up. Although she had her way, a third court case quickly followed as

Wernuro and her son, the scribe Huy, attempted to reassert their right to manage the whole estate. Huy and his mother won their case and retained control over the land. Huy farmed, married the lady Nubnofret and had a son, Mose.

At Huy's death his still dissatisfied family made a further attempt to seize control of the land and succeeded in evicting the young Mose and his mother. Nubnofret started legal action to recover the land. In court she called for the official tax returns to be submitted in evidence, but when the vizier scrutinised the returns he could find no evidence of Nubnofret's inheritance. This was not surprising as, unknown to the vizier, the court officials had been bribed to amend the record. Mose therefore grew up dispossessed of his inheritance.

When he reached maturity, Mose started the fifth and final legal case, submitting a petition to the vizier. Once again the parties stood before the court. Ignoring the official records which he knew to be false, Mose called upon the testimony of the local people, who swore on oath – 'If I speak falsehood then let my nose and ears be cut off and let me be transported to Nubia' – that Mose was the true descendant of Wernuro. Finally, the verdict was reached and the vizier announced, 'Mose is right!' To celebrate his victory, and to ensure that no one else could lay claim to his land, Mose had the whole story preserved on the wall of his tomb. The fate of those who dared to lie before the court is not recorded.

# CHAPTER 3

# OFFICERS OF THE LAW

If the king was theoretically responsible for the administration of justice and the maintenance of *maat*, and the vizier attended to the practical details of the legal system, who actually enforced law and order amongst the people?

We have already met the palace police force, the security guards who protected the king and his property and who answered directly to the vizier. Similar forces were employed to guard Egypt's other state assets. Not only the temples and harems but the borders, mines, deserts and waterways, too, were protected either by soldiers or by specialised policemen who ultimately came under the control of the vizier's office.

The protection of the individual and his or her property was, however, a very different matter. While the élite could afford to employ private security guards, the masses enjoyed little protection against those of evil intent. Throughout dynastic history the authorities remained reluctant to intervene in anything that could be interpreted as a personal matter. The primary duty of the police was at all times the prevention and detection of offences against the state, and any involvement in civil misdemeanours was peripheral to their principal work.

The wronged citizen, seeking justice, was required to play the part of both detective and lawyer. Thus the *Eloquent Peasant*, when robbed, turned not to the police but to the court where he named the guilty party and outlined his case for compensation. In the absence of a police force as we know it today, the community played an important part in the prevention and detection of civil crime. Everyone seems to have known their neighbour's business, and the contempt and ridicule directed at those who violated the rights of others must have been an important deterrent. Public shame, in a small community, can be an important matter.

Egypt never developed a national police force although, during the New Kingdom, the Medjay came close to being recognised as such. The Medjay had originated as nomads dwelling in the Nubian Eastern Desert. Throughout the Old and Middle Kingdoms they had lived on less than friendly terms with their Egyptian neighbours. This had changed at the start of the New Kingdom when Medjay mercenaries fought successfully alongside the Theban royal family to expel the Hyksos from the Nile Delta. The onset of peace saw the Medjay settled in the Nile Valley, intermarrying with the local communities and working as security guards, in which capacity they fulfilled the combined functions of police officers and desert-rangers. A well-regulated, hierarchical police structure soon developed and, as more and more native Egyptians joined the force, the term Medjay quickly lost its original ethnic meaning. Now the Medjay were employed by the state to patrol the towns, deserts and frontiers of Egypt and to act as royal bodyguards.

Even the isolated, purpose-built city of Amarna had need of a police force. Here, in the splendid rock-cut tomb which testifies to the importance attached to his role, we meet Mahu, chief of the Medjay, and see him at work.[1] Mahu is no desk-bound civil servant, but a man of action. Early one morning he is rudely awakened. A report has come in: criminals, possibly foreigners, have been discovered! The chase is on. Mahu leaps to his chariot and drives off, while six police armed with batons and short, forked sticks form a posse and follow their chief. The three miscreants are captured, handcuffed and taken, bent over, before the vizier. Mahu speaks with pride, 'Examine, my lords, these men whom the foreigners have instigated.' As Norman de Garis Davies, publisher of material from the tomb, remarks, 'It is a scene which, in reference to a smaller matter, might be enacted in any Egyptian village today.' A footnote to the publication adds:

> Curiously enough, while engaged upon the scenes, I had striking proof that life in Egypt is little more mutable than the art which represents it. Being called out of the tomb one day by the sound of voices, I found that the police of the excise had lain in wait in the early dawn and had captured two miserable salt-diggers, whom they had driven off to the village, bent double as in the picture; no doubt to go through a similar examination from the village dignitaries in the midst of the ruins of Akhetaten [Amarna]. And yet the world moves!

The officials of Amarna were expected to keep fit. On the back wall of the tomb we see Mahu and fifteen of his men, accompanied somewhat improbably by the vizier and his deputy, as they jog before the royal chariot. This is a journey fraught with danger. Akhenaten and Nefertiti chat, and maybe even kiss, as the king holds the reins of the prancing steeds. Meanwhile their eldest daughter, ignored by her parents, takes the opportunity to goad the horses with a stick. The police presence seems to be a mere formality, however, and it is doubtful that, running as they do with their backs to their royal charges, the Medjay could hope to deter a potential assassin or prevent an accident. Nevertheless, Akhenaten appears to regard his armed guard as essential to his peace of mind. Although generally regarded as a pacifist, he betrays a curious nervousness in his own land. From the very beginning of his reign he surrounded himself and his family with soldiers and policemen, and even his 'agents of the harem ladies' armed themselves with sticks.

At Thebes, the workmen's village of Deir el-Medina was provided with its own band of Medjay, a division of the Medjay of Thebes-West who lived outside the village and reported to the mayor of western Thebes. As employees of the royal necropolis, however, they were ultimately responsible to the vizier's office. The number of Medjay employed in the necropolis varied: in times of peace eighteen was considered sufficient, while in more stressful periods the number was increased to twenty-four or even more. The main duty of the Deir el-Medina Medjay was the protection of the royal tombs which, well-known as repositories of almost unimaginable riches, had to be guarded both from local thieves and from marauding bands of Libyans who might, at times of Egyptian weakness, be tempted to attack. During Year 1 of the unstable reign of Ramesses IV the necropolis journal noted: 'Winter Season, month 1 day 3: No work due to fear of the enemy. The two chiefs of the Medjay came saying, "The people who are enemies have come. They have reached Pernaby and have destroyed everything there and burned its people."'[2]

Of far less importance was the policing of the workmen's village. The Medjay chief did become involved in village affairs, but here he played an administrative rather than a crime-fighting role. He was more likely to be found delivering a message from the vizier's office or sitting as a member of the court than patrolling the narrow streets. Where an official investigation was necessary, the Medjay chief was expected to act alongside the scribes of the vizier and the enigmatic *aatju* officers. These were government investigators, based at Thebes, whose primary brief seems to have been the resolving of high-profile legal problems, principally concerning landed property and tomb-ownership, within the village. These three groups of officials had the added responsibility of reporting any suspected criminal activity within the village to the vizier's office.

Living within the village itself were the 'guardians of the tomb', employees charged with protecting the valuable implements and materials used in the excavation and decoration of the tombs, including oil and wicks, paint, pigment and copper tools. These, as government property, were handed out at the beginning of each shift and collected and counted again at its end. The guardians were recognised as honest men; they served alongside the Medjay as court witnesses and might even conduct low-level official investigations on behalf of the state.

One rung further down the promotional ladder came the 'doorkeepers of the tomb'. These were the security guards who controlled the receipt of government supplies sent from state warehouses to feed and provision the workforce. We find the doorkeepers called upon to act as court bailiffs and even as tax collectors: 'send your scribe together with Iufenamen, the scribe of the tomb, and the doorkeeper Djehuty-mes or the doorkeeper Khonsu-mes. Cause them to go fetch the grain so that the men may not grow hungry and become idle on the work of Pharaoh.'[3]

The Deir el-Medina Medjay chief, in spite of his position, could not always be relied upon to act with scrupulous honesty in his dealings with the workmen. However, private legal actions concerning such an exalted personage are, as we might expect, rare. It seems that a police chief with a complaint against a workman would tend to settle the matter with the aid of his truncheon, while few workmen would wish to take the police chief to court. There is, however, one notable exception to this rule. An ostracon preserves the sorry tale of one Menna who sold a valuable pot of fat to Mentmose, chief of police.[4] Mentmose asked for credit, claiming, 'I will pay you for this with barley obtained from my brother; he will guarantee the deal.' This promised payment never materialised and Menna was forced to take the police chief to court on four separate occasions.

Eventually, the defaulter swore an oath before the court: 'If I do not pay Menna for the pot before the last day of the third month of summer of Year 3 may I receive a hundred blows with the stick, and be made to pay double.' By this time the case was some eighteen years old. Mentmose repaid Menna some two and a half months after the sworn payment date; there is no mention of him ever receiving the hundred blows. Menna, clearly not one to learn by his mistakes, agreed to a complicated repayment schedule. He accepted an ox in settlement of the debt but, as the ox was worth far more than the original pot of fat, he then had to provide Mentmose with a coffin. Menna still ended up owing the police chief sixty-five *deben* of copper, more than twice the value of the initial loan.

Feared far more than the police were the tax inspectors, government officials with sweeping powers to punish and impound. Egypt's fertility made it a wealthy country, but it was necessary to devise a means of physically transferring that wealth from the hands of the primary producer to the storehouses of the king.

> Behold, Yebu and Thinis ... are not taxed because of the civil unrest. Grain, charcoal, wood and brushwood are lacking. The output of the craftsmen and ... the profit of the palace. What use is a treasury without its revenues? Happy is the heart of the king when gifts come to him.
>
> The doleful scribe Ipuwer laments the breakdown of law and order which have led to the failure to collect taxes[5]

Once collected as taxes, produce could be stored and used to pay the wages of the state employees, while also providing a valuable buffer against times of low Nile levels and drought:

> And Joseph went out from the presence of Pharaoh and went throughout the land of Egypt. And in the seven plenteous years the earth brought forth by handfuls. And he gathered up all the food of the seven years, which were in the land of Egypt, and laid up the food in the cities; the food of the field, which was round about every city, laid he up in the same.

And Joseph gathered corn as the sand of the sea, very much, until he left numbering, for it was without number ...

And the seven years of plenteousness, that was in the land of Egypt, were ended. And the seven years of dearth began to come, according as Joseph had said: and the dearth was in all lands; but in the land of Egypt there was bread. And when all the land of Egypt was famished, the people cried to Pharaoh for bread ... And the famine was all over the face of the earth: and Joseph opened all the storehouses, and sold unto the Egyptians; and the famine waxed sore in the land of Egypt. And all countries came into Egypt to Joseph to buy corn; because the famine was so sore in all lands.[6]

The quantities of food stored were indeed, as the Bible suggests, vast. It has been calculated that the granaries attached to the Ramesseum, the mortuary temple of Ramesses II, if ever filled to capacity would hold some 16,522,000 litres of grain, which would support over 3000 families (17,000–20,000 people) for a year.[7] These granaries formed just a part of the total storage capacity of Thebes during the New Kingdom.

Dynastic Egypt could boast three classes of landowner. First and foremost was the crown. Next came the temples, their extensive estates the pious gift of kings. Finally, a long way behind, lagged the private landowners whose families had been granted estates as payment for services rendered. The gathering of Egypt's wealth was the job of the tax inspectors, civil servants working for the chief of the treasury who in turn reported to the vizier's office. As Egypt's economy flourished without currency, any taxes or fines owed to the state could only be collected either as goods-in-kind or as man- or woman-hours. This meant that many Egyptians avoided taxation in kind, either because, like the workmen of Deir el-Medina, they were paid directly by the state or because they did not produce goods suitable for assessment. It would be difficult, for example, to raise an assessment on a doctor or a laundryman.

The regular censuses conducted from the Middle Kingdom onwards suggest that those who could not pay taxes in kind did not escape scot-free; they would be made to pay in man-hours, or corvée labour, instead.

Private landowners and those who rented land would be liable to taxation on the produce of their land, as would the estates of the great temples. Even the gods of Egypt were expected to pay tax, with only those estates that had been specifically exempted avoiding assessment. Amen, during the New Kingdom, was the most prolific of taxpayers. Part of a letter written by the Nineteenth Dynasty lord of the treasury Panehesy to Hori, prophet of Amen, gives us some idea of the scale of his lands liable to assessment. Panehesy had counted Amen's northern assets as follows:

> Cultivators: 8760 men each producing 200 sacks of barley by the bushel.
> Cowherds: ? men, with cattle by herds, each man having 500 beasts in his care.
> Goatherds: 13,080 men ...
> Keepers of fowl: 22,530 men, each having 34,230 birds ...[8]
> Fishermen ...
> Donkey drovers: 3920 men, each having 870 animals.

Each year the tax inspectors and their minions would depart for the countryside where they would measure, assess and collect:

> Let me tell you of the farmer – another hard occupation ...
> When he reaches his field he finds it broken up. He spends his time cultivating but the snake follows him. It eats the seed as he sows it on the ground and he does not see a single green blade ... Now the tax collector lands on the river bank. He surveys the harvest. He is attended by bailiffs [literally, doorkeepers] with staffs and Nubians with clubs.

They say to him 'Give us grain!' but he replies, 'There is none.' The farmer is beaten savagely. He is tied up and thrown into the well where he is ducked head first. His wife is tied up in his presence and his children are bound in fetters. His neighbours abandon them and run away. When it is all over, there is still no grain.[9]

The author of the New Kingdom schoolbook now known as Papyrus Lansing was no doubt exaggerating the farmers' plight; after all, he was trying to persuade his young reader to adopt the best occupation in the world – that of the scribe. Nevertheless, behind the exaggeration lay a great deal of truth. Violence was an accepted part of tax collection and the New Kingdom taxmen set about their day's work armed with a stick with a loop at one end, somewhat similar in style to modern police truncheons, with which to persuade any reluctant payers. In the Theban tomb of Menna, a tax-collector during the reign of Tuthmosis IV, we see the inspectors at work in the countryside using a measuring cord to assess the tithe due. A couple approach Menna, burdened with produce, and pay their due. Others refuse to pay and are summoned to the city where they again appear before Menna to face the consequences of their actions.

Anyone caught interfering with the payment of taxes faced a harsh punishment. As quoted in Chapter 1, King Horemheb had specified that a man found guilty of appropriating the vessel of a person attempting to pay tax would have his nose amputated and would then be deported to the fortress at Sile. It was, however, possible to lodge an official appeal against an over-enthusiastic tax assessment:

One of my workmen came and reported to me that you have calculated an excessive amount of barley as the assessment on my field in the village ... What is the meaning of this? You have decided to pick on me, out of all the taxpayers! So

be it! I am an attendant of Pharaoh, one who is close to his
presence. I shall not be approaching you with my complaint.
I shall approach one with far greater authority.

Nineteenth Dynasty letter from an irate tax payer

All the same, this was not always advisable. Papyrus Mook, a
disjointed document dating to the Eighteenth Dynasty reign of
Tuthmosis IV, tells of the unfortunate case of the soldier Mery
who went to court to determine whether or not his land was
taxable. The verdict went against the plaintiff – 'The one who is
right is the overseer of sealings Sebek-hotep [tax inspector], the
one who is wrong is the soldier Mery' – and Mery was sentenced
to one hundred blows. It would appear that this criminal
punishment was handed out in a civil case as the penalty for the
crime of false litigation and perhaps perjury. We can assume,
although the text does not mention it, that Mery was also required
to pay the outstanding tax.

Casual assaults were very much an occupational hazard of the
lower classes. We have already seen Khun-Anup, the *Eloquent
Peasant*, suffer beatings from both Djehutinakht and the official
Rensi, beatings which he accepts with resignation as in the natural
order of things. In the Old Kingdom rock-cut tomb of the
provincial governor Aba, we see the great man himself 'giving the
order for taking stock of the tomb-estate'. Aba sits, larger than life,
on a stool with a staff in his hand while three scribes prepare to
record the profits of the estate. Behind the scribes we see 'the
bringing of the superintendent of gangs to the great reckoning'.
The reluctant superintendent is forced forward and questioned:
'Tell me what you will give.' On a lower register are scenes of
punishment. A peasant is beaten with a stick and a prostrate man
is held down and flogged by a man wielding two short sticks
terminating in open hands; these curious batons were typically
used during the Old Kingdom to administer beatings. Then a man
who has apparently been beaten is being helped back to his feet.

The accompanying text, badly damaged, states: 'beating is its name, it produces pleasure of heart.' Finally, we once again see the unfortunate superintendent led forward to the reckoning.

Norman de Garis Davies, the publisher of material from this tomb also, was writing at the heyday of the British Empire, when the attitude of the ruling élite to their peasant workers was very different. Nevertheless, he seems to have found the scene disturbing and he bends over backwards to explain what to modern eyes appears quite unacceptable:

> However unpleasantly Oriental the summary discipline used on the official underlings on his estate may appear to us, it may have been extremely wholesome for the peasants who had been accustomed to go their lax way. It would be true to human nature if these little 'foremen of gangs' were themselves the most oppressive taskmasters; and even if the rule of Aba was far from benevolent it might yet be a beneficial exchange.[10]

Davies was in fact echoing the Egyptian attitude to physical chastisement as an appropriate response to criminal activity. The Old Kingdom sage Ptah-hotep expressed it thus: 'Punish firmly, chastise soundly, the suppression of crime establishes good character.'[11] The physical punishment of the weak by the strong may well have been intended for the victim's own good. More importantly it was a time-honoured means of emphasising authority, the élite equivalent of Pharaoh's smiting of the enemy, and Aba includes the scene in his tomb to illustrate his own superior position.

Abuses of power, or over-enthusiastic policing, were rarely reported to the authorities. However, we do know of one instance where the Deir el-Medina Medjay Nakhseti was reported, tried and punished by hard labour 'since he beat with a stick'. The corrupt overseer Paneb, too, was reported to the vizier for mistreating his men. The vizier had Paneb punished, presumably with a beating, but Paneb lodged an official complaint and succeeded in having the vizier sacked.[12]

Sticks and batons, as we have seen, formed a part of the unofficial uniform of both policemen and tax inspectors.

> If an Egyptian of the present day has a government debt or tax to pay, he stoutly persists in his inability to obtain the money, till he has withstood a certain number of blows, and considers himself compelled to produce it; and the ancient inhabitants, if not under the rule of their native princes, at least in the time of the Roman emperors, gloried equally in the obstinacy they evinced, and the difficulty the governors of the country experienced in extorting from them what they were bound to pay.[13]

Higher ranking males, too, went equipped with the staffs or staves that symbolised their authority and which could, presumably, be used as weapons if needed. We do not, however, find the average Egyptian setting off from home armed to the teeth. As far as we can tell, both men and women walked the streets with little thought of attack. It is only during the disruptions of the Intermediate Periods that the sages lament the fact that those who once went unmolested now walk in fear:

> Behold, the land is full of gangs and the farmer goes to plough with his shield ... Behold, the face is pale, the bowman ready, crime is everywhere ... wearers of fine linen are beaten with sticks ... Behold, one runs and fights for a man's goods, he is robbed and all his things are lost ... Behold, things are done that were never done before and the king has been robbed by beggars.[14]

The streets were by no means free of crime, however. Ostraca recovered from Deir el-Medina record a sorry procession of petty thefts, unsatisfied debts and unrestored borrowings (often concerning donkeys). The Old Kingdom tomb of Niankhkhnum and Khnumhotep includes an amusing market scene with a trained security monkey on a leash arresting a naked thief. Yet the absence of money led to an absence of easily portable wealth and so handicapped the would-be street robber. The lack of purses, wallets, handbags and even pockets resulted in a corresponding lack of pickpockets, bag-snatchers and other opportunist villains. The ambitious mugger could only hope to rob his victim of his or her possessions. It would have been easy to challenge an unprotected lady wearing a golden necklace, but much more difficult to make a quick getaway with a squawking duck or a bowl of grain.

Those, like the *Eloquent Peasant*, who needed to travel with their goods apparently did so without undue worry. The obliging River Nile, whose current flowed downstream while the winds blew upstream, made river transport by oar and sail quick, safe and easy for all. Only in the marginal areas which surrounded Egypt, and in the exposed Mediterranean Sea, was there real danger of theft or piracy. Few chose to visit those regions.

# CHAPTER 4

## CRIMES AND PUNISHMENTS

Diodorus Siculus lists some of the judgements meted out by the Egyptian courts, telling us of the laws and punishments which were, even in the first century BC, 'particularly old':

> The penalty for perjury was death; the reasoning being that the perjurer was guilty of the two greatest sins, being impious towards the gods and breaking the most important pledge known to man. Again, if a man walking along the road should happen to see a person being attacked or killed and did not come to his aid, he had to die. If he was genuinely prevented from helping the person he was required to lodge information against the assailants and to testify against their crime; if he failed to do this, as the law required, he would be beaten with a fixed number of blows and be deprived of food for three days. Those who brought false accusations against others had to suffer the punishment that would have been meted out to the accused had they been found guilty.[1]

Diodorus, although mistaken in the details he cites, is correct in his belief that the Egyptians employed standard physical penalties for specific crimes. These physical penalties were, however, reserved for the criminal court. We know from surviving legal documents that the punishments meted out for civil offences, crimes against the individual, generally took the form of correction of the wrong plus some degree of compensation. The punishment was designed to place the victim in a better position than before the crime was committed, while the guilty party was to be left demonstrably worse off. Thus, in the *Tale of the Eloquent Peasant* quoted in the Introduction, Khun-Anup wins his civil case and receives compensation while the grasping Djehutinakht suffers great financial loss.

A small Nineteenth Dynasty papyrus now housed in Leiden Museum helps us to understand how such compensation might be calculated:[2]

> List of the property stolen by the female servant of the charioteer Pekhari:
> 1 bronze wash-basin; 20 *deben*, penalty 40 *deben* of copper.
> 1 ? bronze vessel; 6 *deben*, penalty 18 *deben* of copper.
> 1 bronze spittoon; 6 *deben*, penalty 18 *deben* of copper . . .
> 2 garments of fine cloth; penalty 6 . . .

As the list continues through the vessels and clothing purloined by the hapless servant, we can see that the compensation due is being calculated by doubling or, more usually, tripling the value of the stolen item. Thus the thief would be required to give back the stolen item plus a hefty penalty. An ostracon written in hieratic on a potsherd confirms this policy. Here, although theft is never mentioned, we learn that Lute, a workman in the royal necropolis, has been ordered to pay Hay, his boss, at a compensatory rate of double the original item plus the return of the original item:

> 1 stick, its penalty 2, makes 3 in total
> 1 box, its penalty 2, makes 3 in total
> 4 canes, their penalty 8, makes 12 in total.

Of course, as Egypt was a cashless society, there was a limit to the amount of compensation that an individual might realistically be expected to pay. Savings, as we know them today, simply did not exist, and all payments had to be made either in kind, in metal or in man-hours. This may explain the fate of the thief Khenemes described in a second ostracon recovered from Deir el-Medina: 'when this theft happened, through the workman Khenemes, one took him and caused that he sit at the *khetem*. And he spent 40 days sitting there.'[3] The details of the theft are, however, unrecorded, and we cannot be certain that this was a private crime. Nor, indeed, can we be certain that Khenemes was not expected to work while 'sitting'; his compensation may have been extracted in man-hours.

The New Kingdom *Tale of Truth and Falsehood* is an allegory which, while dealing with issues of sibling rivalry and the righting of a wrong or the restoration of *maat*, revolves around the right of the plaintiff to extract compensation for stolen or, in this case, lost property. Here, however, it was to prove impossible to exact the compensation due:[4]

Once upon a time there were two brothers named Truth and Falsehood. Truth had borrowed a precious knife from Falsehood and, being somewhat careless, had lost it. He had offered his brother a replacement knife but Falsehood was not happy with the exchange, claiming that his own weapon was irreplaceable: 'all the copper in Mount Yal was in its blade, timber from the grove of Coptos was in its haft.' Falsehood sued his brother before the court of the gods, demanding that Truth pay the harshest of penalties. Truth was unable to deny the charge against him and so he was blinded in both eyes and put to work as his brother's doorkeeper. Here his constant presence irritated Falsehood, who soon ordered his servants to abandon Truth in the desert. Falsehood hoped that his blind brother would be eaten by lions. Instead, he was rescued by a beautiful lady who set him to work as her own doorkeeper.

In spite of his blindness Truth remained a fine figure of a man, and some nine months after the rescue the lady bore Truth a son. Many years passed. The son of Truth grew up to be a splendid chap, but he suffered constant teasing from his school-friends who laughed at his lack of a father. Questioning his mother, the son eventually learned the true identity of the blind man who still sat by the door. Shocked at his mother's callous behaviour, the son had Truth brought into the house and made comfortable. Then he talked to him, and heard his story. The son, determined to avenge the wrong done to his father, set off for Falsehood's farm.

The wise son bought a fine ox and left it for safe keeping with his uncle's herdsman. When Falsehood saw the splendid animal grazing in his field he took it, leaving an inferior beast in its place. Returning to claim his ox, the son refused to accept the substitute animal, claiming that his own beast had been far superior to any other: 'There is no ox as big as my ox . . . The Great River is its resting place and sixty calves are born to it every day.' Clearly, no adequate compensation could be paid for the loss of such a magnificent beast. The matter was brought to the court of the gods. Falsehood attempted to ridicule the exaggerated claims made for the bull, but the son of Truth was able to quote the earlier case back at him. In a courtroom drama worthy of a modern soap opera he then announced himself to be the son of Truth.

Falsehood was shocked but rallied to swear that Truth was dead: 'As Amen lives, as the Ruler lives, if Truth is found alive may I be blinded in both eyes and made the doorkeeper in the house of Truth.' The son settled the matter by producing Truth. Falsehood, revealed as a liar, was sentenced to a hundred blows plus five open wounds and was then blinded in both eyes and made to serve as his brother's doorkeeper.

Falsehood is punished with a mixture of criminal and equitable penalties. The hundred blows plus five open wounds are the accepted punishment for the crime of perjury, while the blinding followed by demotion to doorkeeper, not a typical punishment, is a just reflection of the penalty that Falsehood had, years before, insisted be inflicted on Truth.

The state, too, routinely claimed its compensation, variously depriving its convicts and their families of office, property and freedom. In his Nauri decree, Seti I, for example, specifies 'beating with 100 blows plus extracting the property belonging to the House as stolen property at a rate of a hundred to one' as the appropriate, exorbitant rate of interest for theft. As here, financial penalties were more often than not combined with corporal punishments, which became more specific as the dynastic age progressed. By the New Kingdom we find many impoverished prisoners departing to work in the labour-gangs with ears and noses missing.

Beatings, cuttings, mutilations, amputations and executions did absolutely nothing to correct or compensate for crimes, nor did they necessarily encourage the offender to repent of his or her actions, although we might reasonably assume that the noseless criminal would permanently regret getting caught. They did, however, cause the victim to suffer both pain and humiliation, and thus satisfied a need to reassert the authority of the state while providing a dire and permanent warning to others. The gods could see that offences against *maat* would be treated with the utmost severity. No one, having witnessed a mutilated criminal, could be in any doubt that the king's justice was everywhere; no one, having been mutilated, could forget what they had done. Those who were not naturally good might even be encouraged to become so by seeing and imagining the fate of those found guilty of a crime.

Hieroglyphic determinative
for impaling on wood

The most severe penalty that the state could inflict was death
followed by the loss of burial rites. Death provided a cheap and
efficient means of disposing of unwanted and dangerous elements
in a society that had no interest in either rehabilitating its
prisoners or preserving them for years in a costly prison cell.
Although we are invited to appreciate a variety of deaths on the
battlefield – by smiting, piercing with arrow, lance or sword,
decapitation, trampling with chariot and horses, or drowning –
the preferred method of civilian execution was by impaling on a
wooden stake, the convicted party being, in the graphic words of
the Nauri decree, 'caused to fall, he being placed on the top of the
wood'.

The rare hieroglyphic determinative for this type of execution,
as seen in the Amada stela of Merenptah, shows a person
suspended by the centre of the torso on the point of a pole slightly
shorter than the victim (see above). The man is face downwards so
that his arms and legs dangle towards the ground. The point of the
pole does not pass through his back. If this is indeed an accurate
representation of an execution – and we must always make
allowances both for style and for the need to fit the hieroglyph
into the available space – we can assume that the victim suffered
either a very quick death if the wood pierced the heart or a major
blood vessel, or an unpleasant lingering death if the spike was
carefully aimed to avoid those sites. A Ramesside exemption

decree extends our knowledge by detailing not only the method but also the place of execution: 'He who will remove any goods . . . the law shall be applied to him causing him to fall, he being placed upon the top of the wood next to the temple from which he shall have stolen.'[5]

Execution by fire is far less well-attested, a fact that has led some authorities to deny its use as a punishment during the dynastic age. A brief review of the available evidence, however, is enough to confirm that burning, either alive or dead, was recognised as an effective means of eliminating the unwanted at least as early as the Middle Kingdom.[6] In the Middle Kingdom Westcar Papyrus we can read the cautionary tale of an adulterous woman whose unpleasant fate is to be taken to a field to the north of the palace where, at the command of the king, she suffers death by burning; literally, 'he placed fire on her'. Her ashes are then thrown in the nearby river. As her paramour has already been snatched by a magical crocodile – the crocodile being an animal frequently used to symbolise destiny or fate – neither lover leaves a body for ritual burial.[7] The Westcar Papyrus is, of course, fiction, but it is at the very least suggestive.

More specific is the Middle Kingdom Neferhotep stela recovered from Abydos, which threatens burning as the punishment for the inappropriate use of the cemetery: 'one shall destroy him by fire.' The Tod inscription of Senwosret I tells us that those responsible for vandalising the temple 'have been placed on the brazier'. A Ramesside ostracon dealing with the theft of three state-owned chisels announces that those found guilty of such a heinous crime are to be 'thrown in the fire'.[8] The Twenty-Second Dynasty *Chronicle of Prince Osorkon* may be added to this list with its casual reference to the Theban rebels: 'everyone was burned with fire at the place of his crime.'[9]

By the end of the dynastic age burning seems to have become the accepted, although not the sole, punishment for treason or rebellion. The demotic *Instruction of Ankhsheshonq* tells of the unfortunate priest of that name who leaves Heliopolis to visit his old school-friend Harsiese son of Ramose. In Memphis Ankhsheshonq learns the unimaginable: Harsiese has joined a gang and is plotting to assassinate the king. Ankhsheshonq is shocked, and argues in vain to dissuade his friend from such folly. Unfortunately, their conversation is overheard and the conspirators are arrested. While Ankhsheshonq broods on his misfortune in jail, Pharaoh exacts a terrible revenge:

> His Majesty had an altar of earth built at the door of the palace. He had Harsiese son of Ramose placed in the fire [a word that has also been translated as 'furnace' or 'brazier'], together with all the conspirators and every man who had plotted to bring about Pharaoh's doom.[10]

Ankhsheshonq is spared the fiery furnace and survives to write a lengthy treatise offering a wide range of practical advice to his son: 'a man who spits into the sky will end up with spittle on his head'; 'A servant who is not beaten is full of curses in his heart'; 'Do not sleep with a woman whose husband is alive lest he becomes your enemy'.

The texts cited above leave open the possibility that some at least of those committed to the flames may have already been dead, killed by an alternative means of execution. The subsequent burning of the bodies, and the automatic denial of an afterlife, is then an effective means of extending punishment beyond death. We are never told what happens to the remains of those who were impaled. We can, however, guess that they would not be permitted to enjoy the traditional funeral rites; indeed, after prolonged exposure to Egypt's heat, insects and animals, there may have been very little left to bury.

Neither death by impaling nor by burning is a particularly speedy or painless method of execution, although these are certainly not the worst means of official killing to have been devised by humankind. Some, if not all, Egyptian executions were conducted in public places – the Ramesside exemption decree quoted above specifies death 'next to the temple from which he shall have stolen' – where they could serve as a grim and awful warning to those who might be tempted to break the law. As it would have been both speedier and less messy to despatch criminals by less elaborate means (poisoning, suffocating or strangling), we may deduce that the public aspect of the execution was considered to be important. Yet there does not appear to have been the equivalent of the crowded Roman arena or public hangings at Tyburn, and, as far as we can tell, death was not considered a spectator sport. It might, of course, be argued that this is precisely the sort of evidence that would be excluded from the tomb walls, but the more informal records of Deir el-Medina, which detail holidays granted for religious festivals, funerals, brewing beer and coping with hangovers, never mention attendance at public executions.

A reluctance to highlight the execution of criminals in the official records is entirely in keeping with Egyptian thinking. To admit to an execution was to admit that a serious crime had been committed. Furthermore, although the killing of the enemy in battle and maybe even in religious ritual was acceptable, the deliberate killing of one Egyptian by another was understood to be fundamentally wrong. Threats were one thing – Seti, for one, was happy to threaten his herdsmen with the ultimate penalty – but it seems that kings wished to distance themselves from the actual deed. Thus we find Ramesses III, a monarch who is happy to include graphic scenes of battlefield carnage on his temple walls, loudly protesting his ignorance of the severe penalties handed out by his own courts:

I spoke to them strictly, saying, 'Take care, in case you should allow an innocent man to be punished by an official who is not his superior.' This I said to them repeatedly. As for all this that has been done, it is they who have done it. May the blame fall on their heads while I am safeguarded, exempted for ever, for I am amongst the just kings before Amen-Re.[11]

The king is clearly not going to carry the blame for any miscarriage of justice. Those on trial in this instance stood accused of the most heinous offence that an Egyptian could commit. As Ramesses well knew, throughout his reign the penalty for regicide was death.

It seems that the state grew more violent as time progressed, with the clearest and least ambiguous references to corporal punishments and executions dating to the New Kingdom. The extent to which this increase in aggression is a function of the restricted evidence from the earlier periods is difficult to assess. However, the sudden appearance of previously unknown harsh punishments is not entirely unexpected at this stage in Egypt's development. Increasing population, urbanisation, wealth and social stratification, features that characterise the New Kingdom, do tend to lead to an increasing fear of crime against property, which is itself reflected in the acceptance of increasingly violent summary punishments. Increasingly efficient bureaucracy also makes the effective implementation of these punishments possible. Throughout the Old Kingdom wealth had been concentrated in the hands of a restricted élite. During the New Kingdom, with the emergence of a prosperous middle class, people started to fear for the protection of their newly-acquired assets. The same tendency may be detected in other societies, from classical Athens to eighteenth-century Britain, which responded to new-found afflu-ence with a harsh new penal code.[12]

However, it would be wrong to imagine Old Kingdom Egypt as a gentle land of tolerance and non-violence. The Old Kingdom bureaucrats who built their tombs close to the pyramids of their kings did not shy away from the idea of corporal punishment. The Sakkara tombs of the noblemen Ti and Mereruka were by no means the only ones to include scenes of casual aggression towards social inferiors. Violence, too, was routinely threatened to those who might violate the sanctity of the tomb.

At the very beginning of the dynastic age we are confronted with the stark image of Narmer, the first king of the unified country, wielding a mace to strike the foe who cringes at his feet. This is an image that is to reappear time and time again throughout the pharaonic age. The message behind these simple tableaux is clear: violence and kingship go hand in hand. Murder may be wrong, but the king of Egypt is expected, either symbolically or literally, to kill the subhuman enemies who threaten his land. When was the king's right to kill extended to his own subjects? The earliest royal exemption decrees detail financial rather than physical punishments, and we have seen Kings Neferirkare, Pepi II and Demedjibtawy variously threatening loss of income, loss of freedom and loss of burial rights.[13] Are we to understand that these were the worst punishments that the Old Kingdom state was prepared to sanction? Were these specified punishments in addition to, rather than instead of, physical punishments that were so well understood that they needed no elaboration? With the evidence as it stands, there is no means of knowing.

Included in the Westcar cycle of fantastic tales is the story of the magician Djedi who was summoned to perform before the Old Kingdom court of King Khufu:

His Majesty asked, 'Is it true that you know how to rejoin a severed head to its body?'

Djedi replied, 'Yes, that I do know.'

Then His Majesty issued a command: 'Have a prisoner brought from jail so that he may be beheaded!'

But Djedi replied, 'Not a human being, Sire. Surely it is against the law to do such a thing to mankind?'

Djedi has his way. First a goose, then a 'long-legged bird' and finally an ox are brought, decapitated and successfully rejoined. While such fantastic tales must always be read with a degree of scepticism, it seems that during the Middle Kingdom execution without just cause, even by the king, was not acceptable.

Occasionally, however, there might be just cause. The Middle Kingdom *Instruction for Merikare*, a propaganda text supposedly written by an elderly king advising his young son, suggests that by the time of the troubled First Intermediate Period death was recognised as the only possible sentence for those found guilty of rebellion or treason, while lesser offenders might expect a sound flogging:

> A talker is a troublemaker; suppress him, kill him, erase his name, destroy his family and remove all reference to him and his followers . . .
> Beware of punishing wrongfully; do not kill, for that will not benefit you, but punish with beatings and with detention, for thus the land will be set in order. Make an exception for the rebel who has conspired, for god recognises those who are disaffected and will smite down in blood.[14]

There could be no hope of comfort for the rebel after death, and the instruction preserved in the Middle Kingdom stela of Sehetepibre warns us that 'there will be no tomb for he who rebels against His Majesty, and his body shall be thrown in the river.'[15]

The Middle Kingdom Coffin Texts, a collection of spells intended to guide the deceased through the perils of the afterlife, are concerned with the mutilation of the dead by demons or spirits:

> O Lord of the gods, save me from those who inflict wounds, those whose fingers are painful, those who stand guard against the enemy and those who instil terror in the mutilators. They who do not relax their vigil, their knives

shall not slice into me. I shall not go into their abattoir, I shall not sit in their vats, and nothing which the god detests shall be done to me.

*Coffin spell 33*[16]

He will arrive at another doorway. He will find the sisterly companions standing there and they will say to him, 'Come, we wish to kiss you.' And they will cut off the nose and lips of whoever does not know their names.

*Coffin spell 404*[17]

It is not until the Eighteenth Dynasty that the *Duties of the Vizier* confirms unequivocally the court's power to inflict corporal punishment, in this case both the amputation of an unspecified extremity and the administering of a beating, on the living. From this time on corporal punishments or corporal punishment plus financial penalties become the norm for criminal actions, while death plays an increasingly important role in the list of state-sanctioned penalties.

The Eighteenth Dynasty tax-defaulter Mery has the dubious honour of becoming the first named Egyptian known to have been sentenced to be flogged – 100 blows, the penalty for false litigation.[18] Beatings were not intended to be trivial punishments but, as they were often followed by committal to the labour-gangs, we must assume that they were not expected to cause either death or permanent injury. They were often accompanied by the infliction of cuts or open wounds, with both the number of blows and wounds specified. Blows were generally counted in hundreds, wounds in fives. Seti's two hundred blows and five open wounds plus the repayment of working days lost, specified for misappropriating the workforce dedicated to the Abydos estate, appears to be a standard punishment.

Of course, the severity of a beating depends to a large extent upon the implement used and the intent of the beater. In an ostracon recovered from Deir el-Medina we find the policeman Kener swearing, 'if I do not hand over the ox . . . may I receive one hundred blows of an axe handle!'[19] Whether Kener ever envisaged paying this painful forfeit, or whether his oath is an exaggerated way of emphasising his good intent (perhaps the ancient equivalent of 'cross my heart and hope to die'), is not obvious. Few, if any, of the dramatic Deir el-Medina oaths were ever enforced by the court. The breach of contract is clearly a civil offence; in this case, as in many other oaths, the criminal punishment is being invoked as the penalty for lying to the court.

The images that we have of Egyptian beatings show either casual, apparently unpremeditated strikings with sticks, or offenders tied to posts to be formally lashed on the back with slender wands. Some modern commentators have described these official floggings as the 'bastinado'. Technically, this is not correct. The bastinado is a light, rhythmic beating applied to the soles of the feet, a punishment that, if carried out for any length of time, causes severe mental discomfort and swelling not just of the feet but of the whole body. When used to persuade the nineteenth-century tomb-robber Ahmed abd er-Rassul to reveal the location of the Deir el-Bahari cache of royal mummies, the bastinado left its victim with a lifelong limp.

In ancient Egypt, too, beatings might be used to persuade reluctant witnesses to disclose information, or to test the veracity of information already disclosed.

> Examination. The incense roaster Nesamen, called Tjaybay, of the temple of Amen, was brought. There was given to him the oath by the ruler, saying, 'If I speak falsehood may I be mutilated and sent to Nubia.'
>
> They said to him: 'Tell us the story of your going with your associates to attack the Great Tombs, when you brought out this silver from there and stole it.'

He said: 'We went to a tomb and we brought some silver vessels from it, and we divided them up between the five of us.'

He was examined with the stick. He said, 'I saw nothing else; I have told what I saw.'

He was examined again with the stick. He said: 'Stop, and I will tell . . .'[20]

On the wall of the Luxor temple an enormous Ramesses II sits impassive on his throne on the eve of the battle of Kadesh while, below him, two Hittite spies are interrogated with long sticks.

Occasionally these beatings were supplemented by equally simple persuasive techniques. Papyrus BM 10052, an extract from which is quoted above, mentions witnesses being questioned 'with the stick, the birch [or the twig] and the *menyny*'. *Menyny* is a mysterious word which appears to come from the Egyptian root meaning to twist and which carries a determinative implying force. It is occasionally translated as 'the screw', conjuring up images of the European instrument of torture known as the thumb-screw. In fact, screws of any form were unknown in ancient Egypt, and it seems more likely that the word denoted a painful twisting of the arms and feet. Papyrus Leopold II–Amherst provides a helpful description of the questioning of suspected tomb-robbers: 'their examination was effected by beating with sticks, and their feet and hands were twisted.'[21]

More extreme or elaborate forms of torture, such as might be expected in times of short life expectancy and harsh living conditions, seem never to have been developed. Many societies, both ancient and modern, have discovered that the human body with its soft and sensitive outer covering lends itself well to a multiplicity of painful situations. The Egyptians, however, have left no written or archaeological evidence for the use of sophisticated torture, and we have no dynastic equivalent of the rack or the wheel. While it is possible that such matters were kept secret, this seems unlikely. Usually, where such devices are employed they are made known; the first stage in torture at the Tower of London was to show the implements to the suspect, who would often immediately crack.

The end of the Amarna era and the advent of Horemheb saw a hardening of the official attitude towards crime, and an abandonment of the reticence that has hitherto protected us from the harsh realities of the New Kingdom penal system. Now we see a new readiness to spell out penalties in graphic detail. Mutilations, slightly different from those detailed in the Middle Kingdom coffin texts, are to be the official mark of the convicted criminal. Decrees of both Horemheb and Seti provide for the amputation of bodily extremities prior to forced labour. Seti declares amputation of the ears followed by hard labour to be the appropriate punishment for interfering with estate boundaries. Amputation of the nose and ears plus loss of freedom for the criminal, his wife and children is the penalty for stealing cattle. Horemheb, too, follows amputation of the nose with hard labour. Clearly, then, these carefully calculated amputations were expected to mutilate and to humiliate but not to kill. They should not be so severe that they would prevent the convict from working.

Ears and noses were the preferred targets for amputation. It has been argued that these mutilations, inflicted in a community where horrific accidents and disfiguring diseases combined with a lack of medical skills to leave many naturally deformed, would not have had the horrific impact that they would have on our own more sanitised society. However, current suffering tends to focus the mind on the here and now rather than the remote hereafter. So to argue, as some have done, that corporal punishments might be viewed as kinder than the more nebulous punishments relating to loss of office and denial of burial rights detailed in earlier times, might be to assume too much.

The amputation of the outer ear and the nose, although undoubtedly painful, was essentially the amputation of gristle or cartilage with a poor blood supply. There was therefore little risk of bleeding to death. The loss of the outer ear would lead to some reduction in hearing as the sound-collecting features of the ear shape would be lost, and loss of the nose would undoubtedly lead to breathing problems, but, provided that infection could be avoided, the victim would live. The amputation of a hand under the most primitive of surgical conditions would be a far more serious matter. Assuming that the victim survived the shock, loss of blood and infections that would doubtless follow the operation, a one-armed convict would not be of much use to the state.

On the walls of Medinet Habu, the mortuary temple of Ramesses III, are shown grisly piles of severed hands and amputated penises cut from the defeated enemies of Egypt. It seems, however, that these enemies were already dead or severely wounded, the piles of body parts serving as a means of assessing the margin of victory and, of course, impressing those who might subsequently gaze at the temple wall. Living, healthy prisoners were an asset that Egypt was not prepared to waste.

# CHAPTER 5

# LOSS OF LIBERTY

The vizier's court had the power to deprive the offender of liberty and social status, condemning him or her to a life of perpetual corvée as one of Egypt's state-owned slaves. This was almost always intended to be a life sentence. In only one instance do we find the guilty party, the Deir el-Medina draughtsman Nebnefer who has committed an unspecified crime, sentenced to an unusual hundred blows plus ten brands [?] followed by hard labour as a stonecutter until the vizier should pardon him.[1] This ostracon, however, poses several problems of translation; branding, rather then inflicting cuts, is unique as a punishment, as is the temporary nature of the forced labour.

Milder versions of the same punishment may perhaps be identified in those condemned to demotion or loss of office, and those sentenced to pay compensatory man-hours by donating so much of their own (or their servants') time to the wronged party. Seti I, for example, had demanded that those who improperly requisition the Nubian personnel owned by the Abydos temple should suffer corporal punishment plus replacement of the man-hours lost. The records of Deir el-Medina include, 'oath sworn by Paneb: If I cause the vizier to hear my name again [I] will be dismissed from office and I will become a stonecutter again.'[2] The workman Anakhtu, too, was sentenced to 'break stones in the Place of Truth' as the punishment for his assault on three coworkers. At Deir el-Medina such demotion from the work-gang, if permanent, was a very serious matter leading to the loss not only of social and economic position but also the family's government-owned home.

Some families, allowed to keep their liberty, faced losing instead their social position. The Seventeenth Dynasty temple official Teti was discovered committing a serious unspecified crime. His punishment was to extend to the whole family, denying his descendants the right to his office: 'Let him be expelled from the temple of my father Min, and let him be removed from his position in the temple, from son to son and heir to heir, they being proscribed, while his income, his food and his meat are taken away.'[3] We have already seen the Middle Kingdom *corvée* deserter Montuhotep sentenced, 'his being given to the plough-lands together with his people, for ever'. That the loss of liberty could be extended to the wife and children of the guilty party is interesting.

The women of ancient Egypt enjoyed an unusual degree of legal freedom. They were, for example, allowed to own, inherit, buy and sell property; they could live without the protection of a male guardian and could raise their own children. Theoretically, they stood equal with their menfolk before the court; they could bring a case, be questioned as a witness and be charged with a crime. Why, then, in the case of Montuhotep, are the wife and children to lose their independent status? We do not find this punishment in reverse – a man and children condemned for the misdeeds of the wife – but this may be a reflection of the fact that most Egyptian law cases relate to men. It is tempting to see the extended punishment as a means not of denying the rights of the wife and children but of preventing the family from profiting from the crimes of the individual. We have already seen that the state was not averse to exploiting the bonds of the family by holding relations hostage against the return of a deserter; perhaps this is a further manifestation of the tendency to regard the whole family as responsible for the actions of one delinquent member.

The precise definition of the Egyptian slave is a problem that has given rise to much academic debate. The Egyptians themselves used a variety of terms to describe their un-free. 'Dependants', 'forced labourers', 'corvée workers', 'workers' and 'servants' are clearly different types of bonded workers, yet all may be lumped together in translation as 'slaves'. It is obvious that this approach is too unsubtle: ancient Egypt had many different categories of 'slaves' enjoying a variety of rights and working conditions which evolved as the dynasties progressed. While little is known of the treatment of slaves during the Old and Middle Kingdoms, from the New Kingdom onwards we occasionally read of slaves owning property, marrying and even acting as witnesses in court cases. It seems that some, at least, of those who have been lumped together as slaves would perhaps be better reclassified as serfs or tied servants. Those sentenced by the court, however, were definitely at the more extreme end of the scale: their slavery was of the most restricted kind.

Although classified as chattels to be bought and sold by their owners, Egypt's slaves did not lose all human rights. Anyone assuming the position of slave-master was expected to treat his property with an appropriate degree of humanity. While beatings, punishments and harsh work schedules were considered acceptable, outright murder was not. Images of helpless slaves condemned to a horrible death walled up inside the pyramids that they have toiled to build are the stuff of Hollywood fantasies.

Only at the very beginning of the dynastic age do we find some evidence to suggest that servants and slaves might have been deliberately sacrificed to the service of their king. The tombs of the archaic monarchs of Egypt are surrounded by subsidiary graves housing not high-ranking courtiers but members of the king's personal entourage, including his servants, concubines, dwarfs and pet dogs. We do not know how these attendants met their end, but it is possible that they were either killed or forced to commit suicide so that they might continue to serve their master in the afterlife. A parallel may be drawn with the Mesopotamian Great Death Pit of Ur where, in 2650 BC, the divine kings and queens of Ur were accompanied in death by six male and sixty-eight female attendants.

While the deliberate killing of slaves was forbidden, conditions at some of the royal work-sites ensured that few would survive to old age.

> And the taskmasters hated them, saying, 'Fulfil your works, your daily tasks, as when there was straw.' And the officers of the Children of Israel, which Pharaoh's taskmasters had set over them, were beaten, and demanded, 'Wherefore have you not fulfilled your task in making bricks both yesterday and today?'[4]

Those sent to labour on the state-owned farms, or donated to the temples and private estates, were the lucky ones. Those sent on the long trek to the quarries and remote mines knew that they would be lucky if they managed to reach their destination:

> Now one of these days it happened that His Majesty [Ramesses II] was thinking about the desert lands where gold could be got, and thinking of plans for digging wells along the routes made difficult because of their lack of water, in accord with a report made as follows: There is much gold in the desert of Akuyati, but the road to it is extremely difficult because of the water shortage. Whenever the gold prospectors went there it was only ever half of them that arrived, for they died of thirst on the way, along with their donkeys.[5]

Workers who did make it to the camp would be expected to survive with meagre rations and minimal medical care until they too died, far away from the comforts of home and the reassurance of a proper burial. Escape from such a remote site was difficult, and it seems that those caught attempting to flee royal service were treated with utmost severity: 'I found the royal servant Sobekem-hab, who had run away, and handed him over to the prison for justice . . . He will be condemned to death.'[6] The fact that so many swore as an oath of truth variants along the lines of 'If I am lying, may I be mutilated and sent to Kush/Sile/the quarries' indicates just how much this punishment was dreaded.

The woman's oath against perjury, 'may I be sent to the back of the house',[7] suggests that convicted women may not have been banished to the mines, where they would presumably have been of little use, but instead placed in domestic service or in the service of one of the royal palaces or temples. At Deir el-Medina we find government-owned female slaves supplied to the workforce. The slaves, available for so many days a month, were expected to assist in the grinding of corn and other menial tasks; any householder who did not require these services was free to sell surplus slave hours to fellow villagers. The Deir el-Medina domestic slaves were included on the payroll, receiving a modest maintenance allowance, far lower than that paid to the workmen.

Domestic slaves owned by private individuals were, until the end of the Twentieth Dynasty, almost exclusively female. It seems to have been accepted that, amongst their other 'back of house' duties, these women would serve as concubines to their masters. In the tomb of Amenemhat we find a son boasting of the fact that he did not have sexual relations with his father's female servants; whether he exercised this remarkable restraint out of respect for the ladies concerned, or as an acknowledgment of his father's superior rights in this area, is not made clear.[8] Occasionally, a slave woman might be lucky enough to marry a free man – their union almost certainly accompanied by the legal documentation that would confirm the free status of their children, who might otherwise have been considered to have inherited their mother's slavery.

The more sinister potential of female slaves as breeding machines, either for the production of slave-children or as surrogate mothers to the free-born, had long been recognised. Thus the so-called Adoption Papyrus,[9] a document dealing with the affairs of Nenefer and her husband Nebnefer, tells how the childless couple purchased a slave girl to act as a surrogate mother. Two girls and one boy were eventually born, and all were freed and adopted by Nenefer, who then married one of her new daughters to her brother Padiu:

> The stablemaster Padiu entered my house and took Taiem-nuit, the elder girl, as his wife. He is my relative and my younger brother. I accepted him for her, and he is with her now. Now behold, I have made her a freewoman of the land of Pharaoh ...

Those sentenced by the courts, and the children born to them, worked alongside the insignificant number of native-born slaves who had sold themselves and their families into slavery as a means of paying off their debts. They were joined, at the very end of the dynastic age, by a small number of individuals who had chosen to donate themselves to the service of the temple. None of these diverse groups, however, was ever large enough to influence the social structure. Of far greater economic importance, an importance that grew steadily as the dynasties progressed, were the tens of thousands of foreigners captured and 'bound for life' as a result of Egypt's military campaigns.

Many of Egypt's wars, although officially justified by extravagant claims of maintaining *maat* or subduing rebels, were little more than recruitment exercises conducted to exploit a seemingly endless source of free foreign labour. Sometimes there was no pretence: from the Old Kingdom onwards it was considered entirely acceptable to kidnap foreigners – Nubians, Asiatics and Libyans – to work on state building projects. Thus, in a tradition that had started centuries earlier, many of the great Nubian temples of Ramesses II, sited in areas where the raising of a conventional corvée workforce would have been impractical, were built with the help of guest-workers snatched during raids on the nearby oases: 'Year 44: His Majesty commanded the viceroy of Nubia, Setau . . . that he should take captives from the land of the Libyans in order to build in the Temple of Ramesses II in the Domain of Amen.'[10]

Pharaoh knew that he ruled the world. Not only the Nile Valley but also the disorderly foreign lands that bordered Egypt on three sides came under his dominion, as did the Mediterranean Sea to the north and the mysterious regions beyond. Those who lived outside the Nile Valley were consistently despised, not so much for their ethnic origins as for their obstinate and inexplicable refusal to adopt Egyptian culture. There could only ever be one true way of life: the Egyptian one. Any alternative existence was considered highly suspect if not downright dangerous, while any attempt to disrupt or deny the Egyptian tradition was a frightening assault on *maat*. The king, as upholder of *maat*, was required to play a prominent role in the suppression of the misguided foreigner. From the time of the Narmer palette onwards a series of images show a gigantic king single-handedly subduing the inferior non-Egyptians.

In theory, starting from his accepted position as universal king, it followed that anyone, Egyptian or non-Egyptian, who refused to obey Pharaoh's orders could be classed as a rebel. This useful term could be stretched to encompass all, from the Egyptian petty criminal to the foreign soldier, who denied the authority of the king. Thus Egypt was provided with the perfect, theologically sound excuse to impose her authority on all unco-operative foreigners.

In practice, however, this position proved hard to maintain.

Prudence dictated that Egypt could not always insist on her supremacy. Some eminent fellow monarchs, the wealthy and powerful kings of Hatti, Mitanni and Babylon for example, had to be accepted, somewhat reluctantly, as brothers rather than subjects. We therefore find Ramesses II, the husband of two Hittite princesses, writing to his father- and mother-in-law with the greatest filial respect. Back home in Egypt, however, his references to his new relations are not quite so polite. Ramesses, with his customary lack of modesty, had earlier proclaimed a glorious victory over the Hittites at the battle of Kadesh. He dare not let it be thought that the Hittite king was now anything approaching his equal:

> The Great King of Hatti wrote seeking to appease Pharaoh year by year, but never would he listen to him. So when they saw their land in this miserable state under the great power of the Lord of the Two Lands, then the King of Hatti said to his soldiers and courtiers, 'Look! Our land is devastated ... Let us strip ourselves of all our possessions, and with my oldest daughter in front of them, let us carry peace offerings to the King of Egypt so that he may give us peace and we may live.'[11]

Other, less powerful, Near Eastern city-states were tolerated as satellites or vassals. Allowed to retain their own leadership, a policy that freed Egypt from the necessity of imposing local governors, they were expected to show their gratitude and respect by showering their overlord with copious 'gifts'. Gold, precious objects, household goods, brides and slaves were all considered acceptable, and it was well-understood by both parties that a failure to offer this bounty would be viewed as an act of rebellion. Those independent peoples who could not, or would not, pay tribute became implacable enemies – rebels indeed – as did the various nomadic peoples who hovered on Egypt's borders.

To the south and west the situation was somewhat different. Nubia, once an independent entity, had been slowly but surely annexed so that by the New Kingdom it was a southern province to be systematically stripped of her valuable resources. On the western border the nomadic Libyan tribes were regarded with a mixture of contempt and fear but were largely left alone. Only when they showed signs of crossing the border was the army called into action. Then, allowing for Egyptian rhetoric, the reprisals could be terrible:

> His Majesty went forth against them like a flame ... They were threshed as sheaves, made as ashes and thrown down in their own blood ... Every survivor was brought as a captive to Egypt, hands and penises without number. They were brought as captives and pinioned before the royal window of appearances ... Their leaders were rounded up and made into groups and then branded with the name of His Majesty.[12]

Unfortunately, the ill-educated foreigners were not always quick to appreciate the fact that they were bound to be ruled by Egypt. Some resisted Egyptian domination, others first submitted and then revolted. In Egypt, rebels, or criminals, could be processed by the state legal system which, whatever its faults, allowed them the privilege of a trial before sentencing. Foreign rebels, however, were not afforded this luxury. Rebellion met with a swift armed response. In Nubia and along the Libyan border this climaxed in pitched battles which the Egyptians (or so they would have us believe) invariably won.

In the Near East the rebels would typically renounce Egyptian authority and then retreat into a fortified township. The Egyptian army would, sooner or later, arrive and request that the township surrender. If this was accomplished without bloodshed the town might be left intact. More often than not, however, a siege would develop and the town would be taken only after fierce fighting. Initially very bad at dealing with sieges, by the Ramesside era the Egyptian army had developed the strategies and the weapons to make the outcome a foregone conclusion.

There was no Egyptian tradition of battlefield etiquette, no thought of respect for a valiant but defeated foe. The captured rebel township was to set an example to others who might be tempted to follow the same dangerous path. Beneath the stereotyped, boastful phrases and the simple, almost cartoon-like illustrations we see a real disaster unfold as temples, palaces and houses are looted, citizens killed, mutilated, molested or seized, trees cut down, fields stripped bare of their crops.

As the anger and noise of battle died down, a sorry band of foreigners was bound with ropes, laden with the spoils of war and force-marched back to Egypt.

> Let me tell you the woes of the soldier ... When victory is won the captives are handed over to His Majesty to be transported to Egypt. The foreign woman faints on the march; she is carried on the neck of the soldier. His kitbag drops and another snatches it while he is burdened with the woman. His wife and children are in their village but he dies and does not reach it ...[13]

Defeated soldiers, civilian captives and those given by their states as 'voluntary' tribute, or simply sold as slaves, had all lost their right to freedom. All now belonged to Pharaoh:

> I have brought those whom my sword spared as numerous captives, pinioned like birds before my horses, their wives and children in thousands, their cattle in hundreds of thousands. I settled their leaders in strongholds bearing my name. I added to them the head bowmen and the chiefs of the

tribes, branded and made into slaves, stamped with my name
– their wives and children were treated in the same way . . .'[14]

On arrival in Egypt the prisoners were registered and details of
name, parentage and place of origin were recorded. They were
then assigned to a particular government department or temple
and, like Pharaoh's cattle, branded with the name of either the
king or a particular god. It seems that the branding was intended
to be a means of identifying the prisoner rather than a
punishment. On the wall of the Medinet Habu temple we may see
this branding in operation. Several brands are heated in a small
open brazier. An Egyptian official grasps the prisoner by the right
wrist and applies a small thin metal rod to the prisoner's right
shoulder. We have no equivalent scene showing the branding of
convicts, and have no means of telling whether they, too, were
marked as Pharaoh's property.

Those foreigners with any useful form of education or
professional expertise might be allocated to the temples, palaces
and bureaucratic departments where their opportunities were only
limited by their abilities. Others might be assigned, as a reward for
loyalty, to a private household. Most, being ill-educated and
unable to speak Egyptian, were given menial tasks, and we find
foreign prisoners weaving, farming, tending herds, making bricks
and even treading grapes for wine. Amenhotep III boasts that his
mortuary temple was 'filled with male and female slaves, children
of the chiefs of all the foreign lands in the captivity of His Majesty,
their number being unknown, surrounded by the settlements of
Syria'.[15]

A carefully chosen few were conscripted into the Egyptian
army. During the New Kingdom the higher ranking prisoners –
the children of the chiefs who were treated as hostages rather than
slaves – were allowed to serve as palace guards or as members of
the royal staff. Entire groups were allowed to remain intact and
were co-opted as mercenaries, retaining their native dress and

weapons, but now commanded by Egyptians. The Medjay are an obvious example of this assimilation, as are the Sherden, notorious pirates who had plagued the Mediterranean during the early reign of Ramesses II, yet who were a mere five years later to be found fighting alongside Pharaoh at the battle of Kadesh.

A handcuffed prisoner of war is led off to captivity in Egypt (Memphite tomb of Horemheb).

*Left, above and below:* Corporal punishment was a regular feature of Old Kingdom life (Sakkara tomb of Mereruka).

The New Kingdom workmen's village of Deir el-Medina, nestling in the valley of the Theban mountain.

The royal cemetery at Tanis, last resting place of Kings from the Third Intermediate Period.

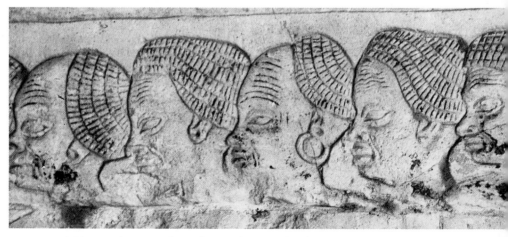

African prisoners of war (Memphite tomb of Horemheb).

*Below:* Seth, god of chaos (New Kingdom block, Memphis).

*Left:* Maat, goddess of truth, order and justice (The cartouche of Ramesses II).

The god Amen being carried in procession (Red Chapel, Thebes).

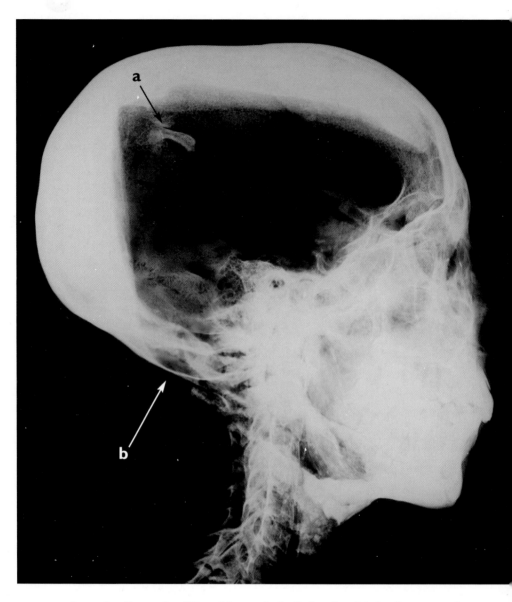

Lateral radiograph of Tutankhamen's skull showing (a) the fragment of bone dislodged during mummification and (b) the site of the suggested blow to the back of the head.

## CHAPTER 6

# REGICIDE:
# THE ULTIMATE REBELLION

The king of Egypt was an acknowledged semi-divine being endorsed by the gods. It was this theology, apparently accepted by all, that allowed him to rule his people with absolute authority. To function correctly Egypt needed her king. His position was unique and unassailable, guarded both by the army and by the gods whom he served, with his divinity perhaps his strongest protection. For most of his subjects, to think of challenging such an august being, to contemplate a direct assault on *maat*, was impossible – the unforgivable heresy and ultimate rebellion combined. And yet, as dynastic history shows, there were occasionally those who were prepared to look beyond the theology, to see the king as a man rather than a demi-god, and to think the unthinkable.

We have already seen the palace police vetted and inspected by the vizier, the conspicuous guard-posts controlling entrance to and exit from the royal dwellings, and the conscientious Medjay running alongside the royal chariot in the streets of Amarna. These very obvious security measures may, to a large extent, be dismissed as so much window-dressing. The presence of the royal bodyguard was intended to impress, to strike awe into the loyal hearts of the people and fear into the evil hearts of foreigners. It may well have protected the king from the odd, unbalanced individual who can be found in any society. The king must have known, however, that the real threat did not come from the general public. Danger lurked far closer to home.

The Egyptians, with their tradition of ignoring that which they found unpleasant, have preserved few details of royal assassinations and attempted assassinations. This is not surprising. To admit that the king was human, and vulnerable, was a very serious matter that called into question the entire premise of divine rule. The two cases that we are able to study in detail, those concerning Amenemhat I and Ramesses III, exhibit a remarkable similarity. Both involve the assassination of a strong, well-regarded elderly king who might reasonably have been expected to die a natural death sooner rather than later.

In both cases the king has already selected the son who is to follow him on the throne. The threat is not to the monarchy itself; it seems that no one was prepared to risk dispensing with a king altogether. Rather, the intention is to tamper with the succession. In both cases the plot is hatched by those closest to the throne, and in both there is a chosen royal successor ready and eager to slip into Pharaoh's still-warm sandals. An earlier instance of plotting within the palace, a harem conspiracy during the reign of Pepi I, is less well recorded but fits neatly into the same pattern.

The pattern is, indeed, exactly what we might have expected to find. To the ordinary people Pharaoh was a remote, august being whose divine right to rule went unquestioned; they would no more think of challenging his authority than they would of challenging the right of the sun to rise and set. It was those with a more intimate view of the royal machine, the wives, children and high officials, who should in theory have been the most loyal of subjects, who were most likely to see their king as a mortal. If no man is a hero to his valet, perhaps no king can be a god to his wife.

From the very beginning of the Old Kingdom the kings of Egypt, unlike their subjects, were polygamous. There were obvious advantages to maintaining many wives, not all of them sexual. The multiplicity of brides served to stress the king's 'differentness' from other men. His prestige, too, could be only enhanced by his ability to maintain a large harem: everyone recognised that dependent women were an expensive luxury that only the truly wealthy could afford. As diplomatic marriages were a good means of cementing relationships with fellow rulers, why be restricted to one? Amenhotep III, a king who famously refused to allow his own daughter to marry a foreigner – 'from time immemorial no daughter of the king of Egypt has been given in marriage to anyone'[1] – eventually wed, among others, two Babylonian princesses and two princesses of Mitanni. These brides were obviously ladies of international importance. They arrived in Egypt, accompanied by large retinues and costly wedding gifts, expecting to be treated with the respect due to their fathers' position. Other royal brides, the daughters and sisters of minor chiefs and local rulers, should perhaps more accurately be classed as hostages whose presence in Egypt would persuade their fathers and brothers to conform to Egyptian thinking.

The ban on Egyptian princesses marrying foreigners, and the apparent but unwritten ban on royal princesses marrying beneath themselves, effectively reduced the risk of problems over the succession by denying foreign or non-royal husbands – husbands who might be tempted to seize the throne on their wives' behalf – to the royal women. The tradition of incestuous royal marriages, while useful as a means of mopping up the supply of unmarried princesses, further protected the succession by restricting the number of royal grandchildren. We therefore find that many of Egypt's queens were of royal blood, being the half- or full sisters of their husband-brothers. Their marriages, mirroring the brother-sister union of Osiris and Isis, served to differentiate the royal family from their subjects while keeping outsiders away from the throne.

The succession was further protected by the treatment meted out to royal princes who, on the accession of their brother,

effectively lost their royal status and had to live out the remainder
of their lives as relatively inconspicuous members of Egypt's élite.
From the Old Kingdom onwards it seems that the royal family was
restricted to the current king, his mother, his sisters, his principal
wife/wives and their children. Princesses, women who derived
their status from their relationship to their father/brother/hus-
band, were allowed to retain their position throughout their lives.
Princes, disgruntled brothers with no obvious role to perform,
were obviously considered too dangerous to have around.

Back at the harem, many wives soon led to many children, a
further source of prestige amongst the child-loving Egyptians.

> Take yourself a wife while you are young, so that she may
> give you a son. You should father him before you grow old
> and should live to see him become a man. Happy is he who
> fathers many children; he gains respect because of his
> progeny.[2]

*From the New Kingdom Instruction of Any*

The prospect of many children brought a virtual guarantee that
there would always be a royal baby available to inherit his father's
crown.

The succession was never the matter of overwhelming importance that it became in some monarchies, and the Egyptians were,
if necessary, content to accept a king who was not the son of his
predecessor. Tuthmosis I and Ramesses I were two successful
monarchs who came to the throne in this way. Nevertheless, the
approved method of accession was for son to follow father just as
Horus had followed Osiris. Consistently high rates of infant and
childhood mortality, however, made the succession uncertain until
it had actually occurred. Ramesses II, the proud father of some
forty-five sons and some fifty-five daughters, can hardly have

envisaged outliving his first twelve sons, to be succeeded eventually by Merenptah, son number thirteen.

Not all princes were born equal. In the royal harem, where all were the children of the king, the status of a child was dependent upon the status of the mother. The sons born to the queen consort, or principal wife, outranked their brothers, and it was ideally from among their number that a successor would be chosen. The sons born to the hundreds of concubines were of negligible dynastic importance and had no realistic hope of becoming king.

The middle-ranking sons, those born to the secondary or lesser queens, were in a more uncertain position. There was just an outside chance, if the king died before fathering a healthy male heir on his consort, that one of them might inherit the throne. How then would the succession progress? Automatically to the first-born? To the king's favourite? We have no means of knowing. We do know, however, that the son who was chosen as heir would live out his life as a demi-god while his rejected brothers were destined to enjoy a life of relative obscurity. The temptation to manipulate the succession, to grasp the ultimate prize, must have been a very real one.

The royal harem was therefore recognised as something of a mixed blessing. Its value as a prestige institution, and as a useful dumping ground for elderly, unwanted and foreign female members of the royal family, was undeniable. However, at times of dynastic uncertainty the combination of ambitious sons and pushy mothers in close proximity could prove dangerous. It can be no coincidence that the royal harem was kept well isolated from the day-to-day affairs of the king's court. While the queen and her children, and perhaps a few royal favourites, were permitted to travel alongside the king as he made his regular, slow journeys up and down the Nile, the majority of the wives and children lived in permanent, rather remote, harem palaces which the king would visit as and when the fancy took him.

Life within the harem palace must have been secure, comfortable, dull and, for the ambitious woman, frustrating. Denied an official voice, each mother must have recognised that her only hope of escape, of achieving the coveted title of 'King's Mother', was through the advancement of her son. While the younger wives waited for the king to call and the older women waited for death, there was plenty of time to gossip, to speculate and to plan.

The classical authors were full of tales of intrigue at the Egyptian court. Herodotus, for example, tells of the planned assassination of his King Sesostris, a combination of the Middle Kingdom rulers named Senwosret and the New Kingdom monarch Ramesses II. The king had been temporarily absent, fighting the enemies of Egypt:

> Sesostris, when he returned home, was received by his brother who had been acting as viceroy in his absence. The brother invited Sesostris to a banquet which he attended with his sons. Then his brother piled large quantities of wood around the building and set it alight. Sesostris, discovering what had happened, discussed the matter with his wife who had accompanied him to the banquet. She advised him to lay two of their six sons on the fire, so making a bridge which would allow the others to escape. Sesostris did as his wife suggested and so, while two of his sons were burned to death, he and his other children were saved. The king then returned to his own land and took his revenge on his brother.[3]

The Egyptians themselves were far more reticent about these matters. Serious offences against *maat* were to be hushed up, not advertised. In consequence we have been left with only enough evidence to confirm that there were at least two, and possibly three, attempted assassinations or harem plots.

The earliest, and possibly least serious, of these occurred during the Old Kingdom reign of Pepi I and was recorded on the wall of the Abydos tomb of Weni, a high ranking official and firm favourite of his king. This wall, a single large slab of limestone, is now housed in Cairo Museum. Weni, whose highly developed sense of discretion forbids any mention of the exact offence committed by Queen Weretkhetes, leaves much to the imagination:

> When there was a secret charge in the harem against Queen Weretkhetes, His Majesty made me hear the case alone, without any judge or vizier, because I was firmly planted in His Majesty's heart and confidence. I put the matter in writing, together with an overseer, even though I was merely an overseer of the tenants myself. Never before had anyone in my position heard a secret of the royal harem, but His Majesty asked me to hear it because he regarded me as worthy beyond any official of his, beyond any servant of his.[4]

Was the queen guilty of attempted murder, or of adultery? No further details are provided and we learn neither the outcome of the investigations nor the fate of the unfortunate queen.

The next indication of unrest within the royal palace is provided by the *Instruction of King Amenemhat*, a lengthy and understandably bitter posthumous letter addressed by the deceased Amenemhat to his son and successor Senwosret I. Amenemhat, the founder of the Twelfth Dynasty, appears himself to have come by his throne by less than traditional means. The new king can almost certainly be identified with the Eleventh Dynasty Amenemhat, vizier to Montuhotep IV. Now it is his direct line that is threatened. Amenemhat first warns his son of the potential treachery of his subjects – 'beware of subjects who are nobodies, whose plotting goes unremarked ... trust no one' – and then goes on to detail the murderous assault that ended his own life during his regnal Year 30:

> It was after supper and night had fallen. I was lying on my bed and resting, for I was weary. As I began to drift into sleep, the very weapons that should have been used to protect me were turned against me. I awoke with a jump, alert for the fight, and found that it was a combat with the guard. Had I been able to seize my weapon I would have beaten back the cowards single-handed, but no one is strong at night. No one can fight alone and no success can be achieved without a helper. Thus bloodshed occurred while I was without you ... for I had not prepared for it. I had not expected it and had not predicted the treachery of my servants. Had any woman ever marshalled troops? Are rebels nurtured in the palace?[5]

It is now generally accepted that this document was written not by the ghost of Amenemhat, nor even by the living Amenemhat having survived the assault, but by the scribe Khety writing in the wake of the king's death. The events described are therefore real rather than fictional. Again, we are left tantalisingly short of clues as to what exactly happened, although it is clear that, if the aim of the assassination was to divert the succession away from the acknowledged heir Senwosret, it failed. There can be little doubt that Senwosret was his father's chosen successor: he had already ruled for ten years alongside Amenemhat as co-regent.

Confirmation of mysterious goings-on at court at the time of the death of Amenemhat may be drawn from the Middle Kingdom *Story of Sinuhe*, an epic tale detailing the foreign travels of a courtier who ultimately discovers that there is no place like home – always a popular Egyptian moral.[6] At the start of the tale Sinuhe is travelling with Prince Senwosret as he returns victorious from a campaign against the Libyan tribes. Messengers arrive hotfoot from the palace to break the news of the old king's death. When Sinuhe hears the announcement he suffers a violent reaction, seemingly out of all proportion to the event. Amenemhat had died an old man, and yet Sinuhe finds that 'my senses were disturbed, my arms spread out and I trembled all over'. Most unaccountably – unless we are to deduce that he knows something that no one else does – Sinuhe decides to run away and hide abroad. He remains in exile for many years, pining for Egypt.

Meanwhile, Senwosret abandons his troops and rushes back to the palace to claim his inheritance. He was wise so to do: a vacant throne might have proved too great a temptation for his junior brothers. It was important to the Egyptians that, just as Horus had buried Osiris, the new king be present to bury the old. The proverb 'he who buries, inherits' seems to have been taken literally. When, during the Nineteenth Dynasty, old King Merenptah died while his designated heir Seti-Merenptah was absent from court, the throne was seized by the previously unknown Prince Amenmesse. Seti-Merenptah had to wait for some four years before he could take his rightful place as King Seti II.

Some 800 years after the death of Amenemhat I came the attempted assassination of the Twentieth Dynasty monarch Ramesses III. The New Kingdom, with its impressive number of scribes, is far better documented than the Old or Middle, and this story is preserved not by veiled references and fantastic tales but by the actual legal documents relating to the prosecution of the offenders. Although once again we are lacking the actual mechanics of the plot, and as always we suffer somewhat from our inability to suggest an exact translation for some of the ancient words used, it is possible to fill in a great deal of the background to events at the palace.

Ramesses III was a strong, ambitious monarch fated to rule in dangerous and uncertain times. A series of population shifts had left the entire Mediterranean world in a state of confusion, with once strong economies faltering. Egypt, although not directly

97

affected, had become an obvious target for those looking for a more affluent way of life. The early years of Ramesses' reign saw three major military campaigns. These were not, as in earlier times, relaxed campaigns designed to extend the limits of the Egyptian frontiers, but desperate wars fought to repel invaders who threatened the security of the Nile Delta. In Year 5 Ramesses fought successfully against the Libyans; in Year 8 he pushed back the Sea People; and finally, in Year 11, came further conflict on the western border. In total Ramesses is reputed to have killed over 30,000 Libyans, an impressive figure which compares well with the 9000-plus Libyan dead recorded for Merenptah.

Away from the battlefield the Egyptian economy was faltering. The worsening international situation meant that trade routes were disrupted. Tribute and taxes were no longer flowing into the treasury. To make things worse there was a bad harvest and inflation caused grain prices to rise. The unwieldy bureaucracy, grown lazy and corrupt, could not cope with the crisis and suffered an alarming decline in morale. Delays in the payment of the monthly rations led to strikes in the Theban necropolis, and sporadic thefts from the temples and tombs, both royal and private, soon followed. The king himself was in trouble, his semi-divine authority challenged by the Theban priesthood of Amen who, already controlling a good percentage of Egypt's wealth, were gradually developing their own hereditary 'kingship' in the south. Now even the royal palace was unsafe, and plots were hatching in the 'harem of the accompanying'.

> It happened because writings were made for enchanting, for banishing and confusing. Because some gods and some men were made of wax ... He was examined and substance was found to every allegation and every crime which his heart had conceived ... These were offences that merited death, and the full abomination for the country was this which he had done. And when he understood that the offences which

he had committed were worthy of death, he brought death upon himself.[7]

Papyrus Rollin, quoted above, and another document, Papyrus Lee, confirm that a band of conspirators, united by a common purpose, had made a failed attempt to despatch Ramesses by magical means, employing wax figurines and spells. Such an approach would be entirely logical for a people who had accepted for centuries the possibility of remote or supernatural killing.[8] Logical, too, was the sentence of death relating to this form of rebellion.

Soon, however, the supernatural was abandoned as the plotters developed a more practical plan. While the details remain obscure, it seems that a coup was to be staged as Ramesses celebrated a religious festival, perhaps the 'arrival of the god', at the Medinet Habu mortuary temple. Ramesses was to be killed, possibly by means of a dagger hidden in a basket, and was to be replaced on the throne by the hitherto insignificant Prince Pentaweret, the son of a secondary wife named Tiy. The Turin Judicial Papyrus takes up the tale with a rather stilted, abridged account of the trial of those involved:

> The great enemy Paibekkamen, sometime Chief of the Chamber. He was brought in because he had been plotting with Tiy and the women of the harem. He had made common cause with them. He had carried their words outside to their mothers and their brothers who were there saying, 'Arouse the people and incite hostility so as to make rebellion against their lord.' And they set him in the presence of the great officials of the Court of Examination. They examined his crimes and found him guilty. And his crimes took hold of him, and the officials who examined him caused his punishment to befall him ...
>
> Wives of the men of the harem gateway, who had colluded

with the men who plotted these matters, were placed before the officials of the Court of Examination. They found them guilty, and caused their punishment to befall them. They were six women ...

Pentaweret, the one who had been given this other name. He was brought in to court because he had been in collusion with his mother, Tiy, when she plotted these matters with the women of the harem, planning a rebellion against His Majesty. He was placed before the butlers in order to be examined. They found him guilty, and left him where he was. He took his own life ...[9]

This was no small or insignificant band of plotters. In addition to the six women recorded above, the judicial papyrus lists some thirty-one male conspirators holding positions of trust: thirteen courtiers, eleven harem officials, five military men and two priests. This list was further extended when some of the trial judges were also arrested, accused of collusion and of gross misconduct with the ladies of the harem:

Persons who were punished by the amputating of their noses and ears because they had ignored the good instructions given to them. The women had gone. They had followed them to the place where they were and revelled with them ... Their crime caught up with them ... The great criminal Paibese, who was then butler. This punishment was inflicted upon him; he was left alone and took his own life.

The punishments meted out to the guilty were severe. Death was the only possible reward for treason. Tiy's fate goes unrecorded, while her son Pentaweret was left to 'die of his own accord', suicide being a privilege offered to very few. The discreet suicide of a royal prince was presumably preferable to his public impaling or burning. Only one of the accused, the trial judge and 'great criminal Hori, who had been a standard-bearer of the garrison', escaped intact with a severe warning.

Unfortunately, in one very important respect, the reporting of the intrigue is less than explicit. We are not told whether the king survived the attempt on his life or whether, after thirty-two years on the throne, Ramesses was indeed murdered. Papyrus Lee suggests that the king, or 'great god', was already dead when the rebels were brought to trial. On the other hand, the opening words of the Turin Judicial Papyrus, although badly damaged and with many unfortunate gaps, indicate that the trial of the conspirators took place during the reign of Ramesses III:

> The King of Upper and Lower Egypt Usermaatre Meriamen, son of Re, Ramesses III Ruler of Heliopolis said ... to bring them to ... before them ... they being the abomination of the land. I commissioned the overseer of the treasury Montemtowe, the overseeer of the treasury Pefrowe, the standard bearer Kara, the butler Paibese, the butler Kedendenna, [further names of judges] ... saying, 'As for the matters that the people (I know not who) have plotted, go and examine them.' And they went and examined them and caused them to die by their own hands ...[10]

It does not, however, necessarily follow that Ramesses lived to see justice done. The trial may well have taken place during the brief period that elapsed between the reigns of Ramesses III and his son and designated heir Ramesses IV. Or it may be that the king, fatally injured in the assault, lingered long enough to convene the court and launch the trial. Ramesses' mummified body shows no obvious wound, but the hardened Twentieth Dynasty linen which remains firmly stuck to his limbs makes it difficult to be certain of this. Poison, often considered a woman's weapon, need not leave any tell-tale signs.

# CHAPTER 7

# TUTANKHAMEN:
# A MURDER MYSTERY?

The very nature of the evidence makes it inevitable that we are likely to learn only of unsuccessful assassinations and failed coups. A king, surviving an attempted assassination, might be tempted to boast of the triumph of justice over evil. In contrast, those who did succeed in removing the legitimate Pharaoh or his heir, diverting the succession away from its intended path, are unlikely to have advertised their dark work. There are, perhaps, some questions we might like to ask concerning the high mortality rate amongst the crown princes of Egypt but these will, for lack of evidence, have to go unanswered.

One negative piece of evidence, however, should be considered before we accept the dramatic image of a corrupt Egyptian court riddled with plots and sub-plots, assassinations and untimely deaths. When Queen Hatchepsut became king of Egypt, effectively supplanting her infant nephew Tuthmosis III, she saw no need to have him killed even though, as he grew to adulthood, he posed an ever-increasing threat to her hold on power. Nor, apparently, did Tuthmosis, having reached an age to rule, resort to killing the aunt who had usurped him. Such remarkable restraint suggests that, at least at the Tuthmoside court, unlawful death was not considered an acceptable option.

One mummy-case that has received a great deal of attention over the years is the postulated assassination of the New Kingdom monarch Tutankhamen. Unfortunately, while those who believe most strongly in the possibilities of the murder theory are happy to commit their thoughts to writing, those who disagree prefer to retain an aloof silence. As a result, this 'murder', like the 'curse' associated with the same king – and, indeed, like the many and varied pyramid theories which seem to emerge every year – has gripped the public imagination. Many now accept as absolute historical fact the supposition that Tutankhamen was killed by enemies who sought to hijack the throne of Egypt. In these circumstances we are perhaps justified in attempting to play time-detective, re-examining the facts for and against murder by person or persons unknown.[1]

> The rest is pure conjecture ... We have reason to believe that he was little more than a boy when he died, and that it was his successor, Eye [Ay], who supported his candidature to the throne and acted as his advisor during his brief reign. It was Eye, moreover, who arranged his funeral ceremonies, and it may even be that he arranged his death, judging that the time was now ripe for him to assume the reins of government himself.
>
> Arthur C. Mace (1923)

Ever since Howard Carter's discovery in 1922 of the golden wonders of Tomb 62 in the Valley of the Kings, Tutankhamen has been regarded as public property. His spectacular re-emergence, soon after a World War and a major flu epidemic had devastated Western society, allowed him to become a splendid and glamorous distraction for a drab and depressed world. This timing undoubt-edly influenced the way in which the news of the discovery was received in the West. Many were reluctant to see his death as a natural event. Even today, by constantly referring to Tutankhamen as the 'boy-king' we are perhaps conditioning ourselves to think of his as an unusually early, even suspicious, demise. In fact,

Tutankhamen was approximately eighteen years old when he died; he was an adult, old enough to have married, fathered two still-born children, and ruled his country for some nine years.

To Egyptologists the story was both clear and simple. Three thousand years ago a young king had died and had been interred in the manner of his people. The tomb and its contents now represented a scientific specimen to be dismantled and examined in order to extract the data which would expand their rather limited knowledge of an ancient civilisation. If anything, the burial was a slight disappointment: there were very few writings, the golden objects were beautiful but essentially uninformative, and the mummy itself was more of a curiosity than a prize find. In the 1920s there was little appreciation of the wealth of information that could be extracted from a mummified body and, of course, many of the scientific techniques that are available to today's pathologists were not yet known. Tutankhamen was subjected to a cursory autopsy by the anatomist Douglas Derry, and then left to rest in his tomb.

Tutankhamen had succeeded to his throne at a time when Egypt was in desperate need of a strong ruler. The Amarna Period, Akhenaten's ill-fated attempt to replace the time-honoured state pantheon with a single deity worshipped via the royal family, had failed after seventeen years. The reclusive Akhenaten was dead, as was his ephemeral successor, Smenkhkare. Tutankhamen, almost certainly the son of Akhenaten by the secondary wife Kiya, took the throne as his brother's acknowledged heir and married his half-sister Ankhesenamen, daughter of Akhenaten and Nefertiti. A new beginning was proclaimed. The immediate past was to be forgotten, the state gods were to be restored and Egypt would once again prosper. As we saw in Chapter 1:

> When His Majesty arose as king the temples of the gods and goddesses ... had fallen into decay ... The land was topsy-turvy and the gods had turned their backs on Egypt ... But

after many days His Majesty rose upon the throne of his father and ruled over the land of Horus. The Black Land and the Red Land fell under his supervision and everyone bowed before his might.[2]

Tutankhamen was, at the time of his accession, approximately nine years of age. To gain and hold the throne as a young boy, to develop and implement such an astute agenda, he must have had strong support at court. Most powerful of all his ministers was the venerable Ay. Ay was an experienced politician who had already served alongside Amenhotep III, Akhenaten and Smenkhkare. Although it is nowhere explicitly stated, there is a great deal of circumstantial evidence to suggest that he was the father of Queen Nefertiti and therefore both grandfather-in-law and step-grandfather to Tutankhamen.[3]

All too soon, Tutankhamen died. He had no living children and so it was the elderly Ay who first buried the king and then took his place on the throne. This, in accordance with Egyptian tradition, he was fully entitled to do. Indeed, Tutankhamen had already taken the prudent step of appointing his step-grandfather as his (presumably temporary) heir, making Ay the official 'Eldest King's Son'. The ancient Egyptians, unlike many modern readers, did not have a problem with a non-royal inheriting the throne; although, under ideal circumstances a son would always follow his father, the harsh facts of life were that no king could be certain of providing a living heir. Ay was by no means the first commoner to succeed a childless Pharaoh. However, it must have been widely recognised that Ay, already an old man, could never be anything other than a caretaker monarch. He, too, had no living son and so, some four years later, we find General Horemheb presiding over Ay's funeral.

The theory, still found in some older Egyptology books, that Ay achieved his promotion by marrying the widowed Ankhesenamen is now known to be based on a set of false assumptions. For a long time it was believed that, for a king to succeed to the throne, he had to marry a royal heiress. This theory, a convenient means of explaining the otherwise incestuous marriages that characterise the New Kingdom royal family, is incorrect: a king might well marry his full or half-sister, but he was under no compulsion to do so. The marriages of Amenhotep III and Tiy, Akhenaten and Nefertiti and, later, Ramesses II and Nefertari show that some of the most successful royal marriages were between king and commoner. The only evidence ever put forward to support the theory of a union between Ay and Ankhesenamen is a ring, of unknown provenance and now housed in the Berlin Museum, decorated with the cartouches of Ay and Ankhesenamen. This, while indicative of a close relationship, such as that between a grandfather and granddaughter, does not confirm a marriage. Ay's queen, as confirmed on the wall of his regal tomb in the Western Valley at Thebes, was his long-standing wife Tiy.

There is, however, some evidence that Ay's reign may not have been greeted with universal acclaim. A cuneiform letter, addressed by a queen of Egypt to the king of the Hittites, sets out the situation: 'My husband has died and I do not have a son. But, they say, you have many sons. If you would give me one of your sons he would become my husband. I could never choose one of my servants and make him my husband.'[4]

This letter is capable of a variety of interpretations. First of all, we have to decide whether it is a genuine appeal for help, or a trick designed to provoke the Hittites (as indeed happened). If we accept the letter as genuine, we must consider the letter-writer. It is most unfortunate that the name of the queen is nowhere recorded. The dating of the letter, however, narrows the field down to a handful of possibilities: Nefertiti, an outside chance as the balance of probability suggests that she had predeceased her husband; Meritaten, widow of Smenkhkare, who disappears without trace at the time of her husband's death; Ankhesenamen, widow of Tutankhamen; Tiy, widow of Ay, again an outside chance since she, as merely the wife of a king rather than a royal princess, would have had little influence on the succession following her husband's death.

Then we have to consider when the letter was written. If the writer is Meritaten, did she write after the death of her husband or after the death of Tutankhamen? If Ankhesenamen, did she really object to Ay, her grandfather, becoming king? Or did she worry about the increasing influence of Horemheb? As yet, we have no answers to any of these questions. This is our last sighting of Ankhesenamen; in the search for evidence of suspicious deaths at court, the sudden disappearance of so determined a lady may well provide food for thought.

So far, then, we have the undeniable evidence that Tutankhamen died young, to be succeeded by the elderly Ay who was in turn quickly succeeded by General Horemheb. Tutankhamen's widow, Ankhesenamen, may or may not have objected to this succession. Someone undoubtedly killed the Hittite prince who, at around this time, believed himself about to become king of Egypt. We must now turn to the physical evidence in our quest for a royal murderer.

Today Tutankhamen's body lies sealed in its coffin in the Valley of the Kings and those who wish to study his remains are forced to rely on the rather scanty reports of earlier workers, and upon the evidence of X-rays taken at a time when the technique was not particularly well-developed. Two sets of X-rays have so far been taken, by Professor R. G. Harrison in 1968 and by Dr James E. Harris in 1978. All who have seen the mummy are in agreement that the king is in bad condition. Part of his chest – the breastbone and the frontal rib-cage – was missing before he was mummified. Since his discovery his head and limbs have become detached, leaving the king effectively dismembered. His corpse is also partially carbonised, a phenomenon that may owe much to Howard Carter's employment of heat as a means of separating Tutankhamen from his nest of coffins and golden mask.[5] It is the badly preserved head that has attracted most attention. Here, in X-ray, it is possible to see a detached fragment of bone within the skull; this is, however, a false clue, and it is now generally agreed that it is the result of post-mortem damage.

Of considerably greater interest is an area of darkness or thickening observable at the base of the skull just where the head joins the neck. Although R. G. Harrison, late Professor of Anatomy at Liverpool University, believed this area of density to be within the accepted normal range, a diagnosis with which no one has yet quarrelled, there exists the possibility that it may indicate a haemorrhage. This putative haemorrhage, the result of a blow to the back of the head, may well have been serious enough to cause death. However, an area of clouding in the region of the thickening may or may not be evidence for a calcified membrane formed over the blood clot. If it is a membrane, it complicates the issue by suggesting that the king may have lived for at least two months, and possibly far longer, after receiving the blow. This means that the blow, even if it existed, may have had nothing to do with the king's untimely death.

Here the speculation really starts. The putative haemorrhage is in a position that makes it unlikely to have been caused by a simple fall. Violence, be it deliberate or accidental, seems to be indicated. Is this sufficient evidence to substantiate a claim of murder? The wound itself is in a difficult position. The king must have been attacked from behind, perhaps, as Dr Bob Brier suggests, 'while he was sleeping on his side or back'.[6] Dr Brier is presumably acknowledging here the difficulty of envisaging Tutankhamen sleeping on his front using the traditional hard Egyptian head-rest. However, to strike a person lying on a low bed and partially protected by a curved head-rest would have been difficult and, indeed, almost impossible if the king was lying on his back. The more obvious and certain approach, given that the wound was bound to be discovered, would have been to bring the weapon down to smash the top of the skull.

Could the haemorrhage be the result of an accident, perhaps the unfortunate result of a chariot, boating or horse-riding misadventure? Statistics would indicate that this is more likely to be the case. Accidents are far more common than murders and, even in our modern, safety-conscious society, accidents are the greatest cause of involuntary death among young males. The preserved medical papyri, handbooks detailing the treatment of common injuries and illnesses, confirm that head-wounds were an all-too-frequent feature of ancient Egyptian life.

The Edwin Smith Surgical Papyrus is the most helpful in this respect, detailing a series of traumatic injuries and concentrating on wounds to the head.[7] This describes, for example, 'a wound in the head, penetrating to the bone', 'a gaping wound in the head penetrating to the bone', and an even more serious wound actually splitting the skull:

> When you examine a man showing a gaping wound on his head, penetrating to the bone and splitting the skull, you should palpitate the wound. If you can feel something disturbing under your fingers, and the patient shudders excessively, while the swelling which is over it protrudes, and he discharges blood from both his nostrils and from both his ears, and he suffers with stiffness in the neck so that he is unable to look at his two shoulders and his breast ... you shall say regarding this patient: 'An ailment with which I will contend.'

In addition, the damage to Tutankhamen's chest, generally overlooked in the murder theory, lends some support to the accident hypothesis (assuming that it is not simply the result of post-mortem damage in the undertaker's workshop).

To summarise the physical evidence: we are faced with a young man who might have sustained a blow to the head which might have killed him. The blow may have been deliberate or accidental.

In the tradition of the best detective fiction, we should now consider our suspects. Who benefited from the death of the king? If we rule out the possibility of an anonymous assassin acting alone with an unknown motive, the field of potential murderers is surprisingly narrow. Ankhesenamen is highly unlikely to have killed her husband: her position was entirely bound up with his and she lost rather than gained by his death. Either Ay or Horemheb could have killed him – they, as the principal beneficiaries must be considered the obvious suspects – and yet it is hard to imagine these two powerful men first working to establish the king on his throne and then removing him by such obvious means. Would not Ay and/or Horemheb have struck following the death of Akhenaten, or of Smenkhkare? Why use a blow to the head, when murder by poisoning or smothering would almost certainly have gone undetected? As we have already seen, regicide was acknowledged as a heinous crime which, when discovered, should not be allowed to go unpunished. If his predecessor had been killed – even at his own command – would not Ay have presided over the trial of his henchmen?

Until these questions can be answered, or perhaps until the mummy of Tutankhamen is re-examined using modern analytical techniques, we can progress no further in our search for the truth. Somewhat regretfully, for a murder-mystery is always of interest even if it is some 3000 years old, we must record a verdict of 'not proven' on the charge of murder.

CHAPTER 8

# THE SECOND OLDEST
# PROFESSION

Why did the ancient Egyptians work, and in some cases steal, to obtain ever greater riches? For many the answer was obvious. Just like the modern reader, they were forced to work to provide for their families and to store up surpluses against times of shortage, illness and old age. Others, those blessed with inherited wealth or position, strove to acquire life's luxuries: better food and drink, better housing, better clothing, and, last but by no means least, better funerary provisions. The proper furnishing of the tomb was, throughout the dynastic age, seen as a matter of grave importance.

We have already encountered the firmly-held Egyptian belief that if the body managed to survive within its tomb a form of the spirit, known as the Ka, could also cheat death and live for ever. It was this belief which led to the centuries-long quest for an infallible method of preserving the corpse, and which made punishments involving the destruction of the body all the more awful. Life beyond death, however, meant different things to different people at different times.

During the Old Kingdom, Pharaoh was the only Egyptian who could hope to enjoy any form of afterlife away from the tomb. Released, his spirit might sail high in the sun boat of Re, or dwell in the Field of Reeds with Osiris. Back in Egypt, his courtiers would also survive but they would be for ever confined to the gloom of the tomb. Not unreasonably, Egypt's élite did not relish the thought of an eternal life spent in the cramped and sandy confines of the simple pit grave which, throughout the dynastic era, served the majority of the population well. It was felt that the Ka of the nobleman needed a more elegant, roomy home – a private chamber to house the mummified body and its preserved organs, plus an offering chamber which would allow the deceased to interact with the visitors who, it was hoped, would bring offerings to the tomb. Storage space, too, was important. As the Ka would need access to all the worldly goods which would allow a pleasurable life after death, the earliest private tombs were filled with an impressive array of consumer items ranging from the prosaic – food, drink, linen and even occasionally a lavatory – to the luxurious – jewellery, perfumes, cosmetics and games with which to while away eternity.

Towards the end of the Second Dynasty came the realisation that it would never be possible to equip the dead with sufficient grave goods to last for ever. But how could the Ka survive, denied its supply of food and drink? A viable alternative to the wholesale provision of goods at the time of the funeral was the employment of a Ka priest. The priest and his descendants, funded by an endowment of land, could be relied upon to make offerings to the deceased for all eternity (or at least for as long as the endowment lasted). Cheaper and more reliable, however, was the use of magic. Symbolic funerary goods and even miniature servants could be incorporated in the tomb in the form of pictures or models which would, after the funeral, magically spring to life and set to work for their dead master. From the Third Dynasty onwards, private tombs were redesigned to include large expanses of wall where images could be painted or engraved. Initially these were concerned with the material goods that would be needed by the spirit within the tomb. Later, as the Field of Reeds opened its gates to all, scenes of the deceased and his family enjoying life with Osiris grew popular.

The Middle Kingdom saw a gradual relaxing of the strict rules of entry to the afterlife. First Egypt's élite, and then her middle classes, assumed the right to leave the close confines of the tomb. Their spirits too would now embark on the long adventure that led to the Field of Reeds; their hearts would face the last judgement in the court of Osiris. For this most important of journeys the newly liberated dead would need the appropriate equipment. Sales boomed as scribes, soldiers and accountants, Egypt's *nouveaux riches*, started to aspire to the full paraphernalia of Egyptian death: the mummified bodies, golden grave goods, illustrated papyri and wooden coffins which had hitherto been the preserve of the king and his immediate court. No longer could Pharaoh threaten to exclude his followers from the royal necropolis; proximity to the king in death had lost its perceived value and provincial graveyards flourished.

The tradition of bulk-burying practical household items in private graves had by this time largely ceased although kings, following the old traditions, were provided with a mixture of ritual items for use in the next world and consumer goods intended for use within the grave. Having seen the wonders of Tutankhamen's small and insignificant tomb, we can only guess at the funeral equipment prepared for the wealthiest and longest-lived Pharaohs such as Amenhotep III or Ramesses II.

Lesser mortals were buried with more modest paraphernalia, again a mixture of the practical, the personal and the ritual. At Thebes the Eighteenth Dynasty tomb of the royal architect Kha and his wife Merit included standard funerary items (coffins, shabti figures and a statue of the deceased) plus many personal goods. In addition to items of furniture and food, Kha had his own toilette set, writing palette, drill, axe, scalpel, drinking cups and strainers, clothing and shoes; Merit had a wig, comb, bronze needles and alabaster perfume vases. This impressive assemblage is now housed in the Egyptian Museum of Turin.

The dead, substantially more wealthy than many of the living, were at all times vulnerable to the more unscrupulous members of

Egyptian society who were happy to prey upon the bereaved and deceased. In the Middle Kingdom the scribe Ipuwer bemoaned the fate of the desecrated dead when law and order collapsed at the end of the Old Kingdom:

> Behold, hearts are violent and pestilence stalks the land; blood is everywhere and there is no shortage of death. The shroud calls out before one comes near it. Behold, many dead are buried in the river. The stream becomes the grave and the tomb becomes a stream ... Behold, rich and poor say, 'I wish I were dead!' while little children wail, 'He should not have caused me to live.' Behold, the children of the princes are dashed against the wall and babies are put out on high ground. Behold, those who were entombed are cast on high ground and the embalmers' secrets are thrown away.[1]

Morally, robbing or abusing the dead was indefensible – Ipuwer is shocked when it occurs – and yet there were many who were prepared to breach this taboo; and the long-standing tradition of including valuable artefacts within the tomb led naturally to the equally long-standing tradition of tomb-robbing, 'Egypt's second oldest profession'. The ubiquitous tomb- and grave-robbers posed a constant threat to the Egyptian way of death. Already active in the pre-dynastic era, they continued their dark work throughout and well beyond the dynastic age. Indeed, there are some who would argue that today's archaeological missions to the Valleys of the Kings and Queens are little more than the officially sanctioned exploitation of the dead.

Legends suggest that even the highest born might be tempted to rob the dead, and that even they would be expected to pay a high price for their crime. Prince Khaemwaset, fourth son of Ramesses II, was revered after his death as the semi-mythological wise man, Setne Khaemwaset. Today, just two papyri preserve fragments of the cycle of fantastic Setne tales: *Setne 1* is written on a Ptolemaic papyrus housed in Cairo Museum, and *Setne 2* on a Roman papyrus in the British Museum.[2] *Setne 1* tells how Setne determines to use his powers to steal the magical Book of Thoth from its guardian, the dead priest Naneferkaptah, who had himself perished attempting to steal the book. The two play a game of senet and the game ends with the victorious Setne in possession of the book.

Tomb-robbers, however, can never be allowed to profit from their crime. Now Setne's life takes a sharp downturn as he is ensnared by the evil Tabubu and persuaded to sacrifice his children for one night of passion. Tabubu and Setne celebrate as the bodies of the children are eaten by dogs and cats. Then the couple lie down together, but as Setne reaches out towards Tabubu she lets out an awful scream. Setne wakes up to find himself naked and alone in the desert. Fortunately, his father happens to be riding by. Ramesses stops and advises his son to return the book. This Setne does, ensuring that the tale has a happy ending.

Crime, in all too many cases, started at the undertakers' workshop. Here the recently deceased would be sent to be washed, eviscerated, dried and bandaged. In Egypt's hot, fly-ridden climate it was sensible to take the body to the undertaker as quickly as possible. Yet, if we believe Herodotus, there were some who thought it prudent to keep their female relatives at home for a day or so:

> The wives of men of rank are not given to be embalmed immediately after death, nor indeed are any of the more beautiful and valued women. It is not until they have been dead three or four days that they are carried to the embalmers. This is done to prevent indignities from being offered them. It is said that once a case of this kind occurred; the man was detected by the information of his fellow workmen.[3]

Necrophilia, if not a crime, was certainly considered a moral outrage.

The mysteries of mummification, a religious as well as a practical rite, were kept well hidden from the general public. The bereaved family, having submitted the dear departed to the care of the undertaker, would some seventy days later be presented with a neatly wrapped parcel, a box of entrails and a steep bill. Who could confirm that this stiff and shrouded package was indeed the same body, that the correct materials had been used, that the proper amulets and jewels – necessary to protect the deceased on the long journey to Osiris – had been placed on the lifeless limbs? The client had to take all these matters and more on trust, and the opportunities for malpractice within the embalming workshop were legion. Today, with the benefit of modern science, we are able to peek beneath the neat bandages and glimpse the bones below. We now know that some apparently perfect mummies, particularly those dating to the Late and Graeco-Roman Periods, house not one carefully embalmed corpse, but a jumbled mass of bones and rubbish.

The funeral, too, offered valuable opportunities to the dishonest. Gravediggers, preparing for a new interment, might stumble across and loot an old tomb. State employees, excavating a royal tomb, might cut into an earlier burial thus gaining access to its treasures. Undertakers, sealing a mummy in a family vault, might well be tempted to help themselves before bolting the door. Indeed, it seems likely that the locking coffin, a Middle Kingdom invention, was developed to protect the mummy from the casual rifling of the funeral director, as it was unlikely to keep the more determined tomb-robber out. In at least one instance we know that worthless pieces of wood were substituted for the valuables that should have been stored in a sealed jewellery box. Unfortunately, the more thorough looting of the later tomb-robbers tends to obscure the evidence of these earlier petty crimes.

The clearest preserved example of undertakers, or even funeral guests, stealing from the dead comes from the burial of the Twenty-first Dynasty Princess Henttawi, daughter of the high priest Pinudjem. Henttawi had been interred in a vault the wooden door of which allowed subsequent mummies to be added. Her burial was followed by that of Princess Djedmutesankh and then by that of another Henttawi. During the funeral of Henttawi II, while the new arrival lay undisturbed in her coffin, the other two bodies were attacked in what appears to have been a hurried search for valuables. The thieves, anxious to conceal the evidence of their crime, then pulled the outer shrouds over the mummies before departing, bolting the door behind them. When a fourth mummy, Menkheperre, was added to the collection, thieves, throwing caution to the wind, cut the gilded faces off the three earlier coffins. Subsequent archaeological investigation was to confirm that Henttawi II had been robbed even before she reached the vault. Her outer bandages presented an orderly appearance but beneath them was disorder. Her mummy jewellery had disappeared, leaving ghostly traces in the resin used in the embalming process.

All ceremonies over, the deceased was laid to rest and the funeral guests departed. The tombs of the kings and queens, well protected by guards and priests, might remain intact for decades or even centuries. More humble burials, however, were most likely to be attacked immediately after the funeral, before the tomb or grave was forgotten. Indeed, palaeopathological examination of human remains in the Riqqeh cemetery shows that in some cases the displaced bodies were still flexible – and therefore very recently buried – when cast aside by the thieves. Here it is apparent that the robbers worked in a systematic manner, carefully targeting the wealthy interments and marking the robbed tombs so that no one would waste time attempting to re-enter them.

This confirms what we might have already suspected: in all too many cases the robbers were those intimately connected with the functioning of the cemetery. The workmen who built the élite tombs, the gravediggers who worked in the public graveyards, and even the guards and priests employed to protect the dead – all were tempted to profit from their specialised knowledge. With their inside information concerning the contents of the graves plus their well-honed skills as labourers, tunnellers and stonemasons, local cemetery officials were able to target those burials that offered the richest pickings. It was not unknown for thieves to burrow unobserved from one wealthy burial to another, leaving the poorer interments untouched. Furthermore, they knew exactly who could be bribed to look the other way. Those graves that did survive intact were either those too poor to merit the attention of the thieves, or those that were accidentally hidden. In the case of Tutankhamen, the best-known example of a virtually intact royal burial, the tomb doorway had been concealed by a rubbish dump created during the excavation of the tomb of Ramesses VI. Even so, thieves had already managed to breach tomb security on two separate occasions.

The thieves were selective in their choice of loot. Metal, textiles, wood, ivory and papyrus were consistently desirable; cosmetics and unguents, items with a limited viability, were only taken from the more recent graves; pottery was smashed rather than stolen. Unfortunately, the jewellery and amulets wrapped within the bandages, being valuable, portable, easy to hide and easy to recycle, made the mummy itself highly vulnerable to attack. This mummy jewellery was considered an essential element of the funerary ritual; no one was prepared to risk abandoning the protective charms that would help them on the arduous journey to the Field of Reeds. In consequence, successful robbers would head straight for the mummy, which would be hacked to pieces in the search for ornaments.

Throughout the dynastic age the élite struggled to overcome the problem posed by tomb-robbers without abandoning their belief in the need for large-scale tombs, bejewelled corpses and copious grave goods. Secrecy was obviously the best form of defence, but in the necropolis secrecy proved impossible. The earliest Old Kingdom monarchs and their courts had built themselves mastaba tombs, which consisted of a sunken burial chamber topped by a conspicuous rectangular mud-brick superstructure providing extensive storage facilities. Already, by the Second Dynasty, the easily accessible store-rooms were attracting thieves, and it proved prudent to simplify the superstructure, replacing the above-ground storage with subterranean chambers cut into the cemetery bedrock.

By the time that the Third Dynasty king Djoser broke with tradition to build his step-pyramid complex, many of the early royal graves had already been plundered and Djoser, salvaging what he could, included both artefacts and human remains from the tombs of his ancestors within his own tomb. From now onwards the kings of the Old and Middle Kingdoms, for sound theological reasons, built highly visible pyramids surrounded by temple and administrative buildings plus the smaller pyramids of their queens and the tombs of their courtiers. No one could hide these complexes; no one wanted to try. The pyramid, in all its glory, was designed to be seen. Massive, cased in gleaming white limestone and capped with glittering gold, it sparkled in the Egyptian sunlight, dominating a landscape where high-rise build-ings were otherwise unknown. In so doing it served as a signpost to untold hidden treasures.

If the pyramid could not be kept secret, perhaps the route to the burial chamber could be hidden? The royal architects experi-mented with a variety of physical barriers, incorporating intriguing combinations of hidden entrances, false chambers, stone portcul-lises and back-filled corridors in their designs. Most ingenious of all was the Hawara pyramid of Amenemhat III, where a system of sliding trap-doors and false passages lead to a seemingly impene-trable burial chamber carved from a single, massive block of quartzite and accessible only from the roof. Unfortunately, the trap-doors so carefully planned by the architect had been left open by the builders, and although signs of abortive tunnelling in the false passages indicate that the robbers had at first been puzzled by the pyramid, the security devices merely served to delay the inevitable.

The rewards of success were great, and the thieves – all too often those who had built the defences in the first place – were prepared to risk life and limb spending many hours tunnelling around obstructions and through fills. The discovery of a squashed robber in the Riqqeh cemetery, caught by a rock-fall and represented only by a pair of skeletal arms reaching out towards his victim plus a heap of bones on the floor nearby, serves to emphasise just how dangerous such activities could be.

If physical barriers failed, what else could be provided to protect the corpse? The solution beloved of the modern movie industry – the death of everyone connected with the design and building of the pyramid – was not one that the Egyptians chose to explore. Magic – the provision of spells to guard the deceased – proved to be a spectacularly ineffective measure. Nevertheless, in a triumph of hope over experience, the builders continued to include protective spells within their tombs, threatening dire consequences for those who might be tempted to violate or destroy: 'Let the crocodile be against him in the water, the snake be against him on land. If anyone acts against this tomb it will not be I who acts against him, but God himself who judges him.'4 The tomb-robbers, possibly illiterate and certainly not deterred, pressed on regardless.

The tomb of the nomarch Ankhtify at Mo'alla, Upper Egypt, includes remarkable descriptions of life during the unsettled First Intermediate Period. Here we read of civil war, of famine and even of cannibalism, and here, too, we learn of the punishment that awaits those who might be tempted to desecrate the tomb:

> With regard to any ruler who will rule in Mo'alla and who will commit an evil act against this coffin or against any part

of this tomb, his arm will be cut off for Hemen during his procession ... and Hemen will not accept his meat offering ... and his heir will not inherit from him.[5]

Hemen is the local falcon god, a variant of Horus. While it remains an outside possibility that the violator will simply be required to sacrifice an ox to Hemen, the translator of this text, Harco Willems, is firmly of the view that the offender will himself be sacrificed to the god as the climax of a ritual procession. He compares the text to the designated punishment for those who steal offerings detailed in the Elephantine stela of Sarenput I: 'his arm shall be cut off, his neck will be severed like that of a bird, his position will no longer exist ... he is destined for the fire.' These are, of course, mere words, and we have no evidence that the state or local court would uphold such violent threats.

The burial equipment of Queen Hetepheres gives some indication of the scale of the treasure that was attracting the thieves to the pyramids. Hetepheres was the mother of Khufu, or Cheops, builder of the Great Pyramid of Giza.

the wickedness of King Cheops [Khufu] was such that, when he had spent all his treasures and wanted more, he sent his daughter to the brothels with orders to procure for him a certain sum – how much I cannot say, for I was not told. This she managed to do. At the same time, bent on leaving a monument to perpetuate her own memory, she obliged each customer to make her a present of a stone towards the works that she contemplated. With these stones she built the pyramid that stands midmost of the three that are in front of the Great Pyramid.[6]

In 1925 part of Queen Hetepheres's funerary equipment was discovered stored in a chamber at the base of a blocked shaft close by the Great Pyramid. Included within the chamber were an alabaster sarcophagus, an alabaster canopic box containing the queen's organs, and a collection of furniture and pottery including an elegant golden canopy (dismantled), a bed, a carrying chair and two sitting chairs. Many of the items were broken and there was no sign of the queen's body, suggesting that this was a reburial of items salvaged after the queen's original tomb had been robbed.

The richness of Hetepheres's burial may be contrasted with the altogether poorer assemblage provided for Queen Iput, wife of the Sixth Dynasty king Teti and mother of Pepi I. Although thieves had made their way into her tomb in antiquity, Iput's skeleton was discovered intact, lying in a cedar coffin within a limestone sarcophagus. The remains of a gold necklace, a bracelet and, curiously, five canopic jars were recovered.

As the New Kingdom dawned, over a thousand years after the reign of Khufu, the pyramids lay empty and abandoned, the bodies of the once-mighty Pharaohs, their queens and their courtiers long since destroyed. The pyramid complexes were in such a state of disorder that Prince Khaemwaset, son of Ramesses II, resolved to put matters right, thereby earning himself the title of the world's first Egyptologist.

> It is the high priest of Ptah, the sem-priest, Prince Khaemwaset, who has perpetuated the name of the king ... Very greatly did the sem-priest Prince Khaemwaset desire to restore the monuments of the kings of Upper and Lower Egypt, because of what they had done, the strength of which monuments was falling into decay.[7]

Pyramids were no longer in fashion. The Eighteenth Dynasty Theban royal family, founders of the New Kingdom and devotees of the god Amen, had taken advantage of the theological shift occasioned by their accession to introduce a new style of royal tomb. Abandoning the conspicuous pyramid complex, they split the tomb into its two constituent parts. From now on there would be a highly visible mortuary temple situated on the west bank of the River Nile opposite Thebes plus an entirely separate tomb cut deep into the rock of the Theban mountain. The vital offerings to the deceased could be made at the mortuary temple, while religious requirements could be satisfied by the mountain itself serving as a symbolic pyramid rising above the hidden grave.

The new royal necropolis was well chosen. The Valleys of the Kings and Queens were remote, mysterious places far off the beaten path. As such they were relatively easy to guard. Ineni, architect of Tuthmosis I, the first king to lie in the Valley, tempted fate by boasting that he had successfully built his master's tomb 'none seeing, none hearing'. Unfortunately, time was to prove Ineni wrong.

The pyramids had been built by thousands of temporary labourers summoned under the corvée system. While it is impossible to be precise, a figure of some 20,000–30,000 working in three-month stints for perhaps as long as twenty years seems possible.[8] This, too, was to change. The enclosed, intimate conditions of the rock-cut tomb called for a smaller and more specialised gang of labourers. By the time of Horemheb the advantages of a permanent workforce had been recognised. Now the 'Servants in the Place of Truth', as the royal tomb-workers were known, were full-time state employees chosen by, and accountable to, the vizier, their loyalty guaranteed by their generous pay and by an oath of allegiance sworn at the time of their appointment. They, together with their families, were compelled to live in Deir el-Medina, a purpose-built housing complex initially founded to accommodate the more transient labourers employed on the Eighteenth Dynasty royal tombs. Here the houses were all owned by the state and appointment to a place in the work-gang was accompanied by the allocation of a tied home.

This government ownership meant that the families of the workmen, and in particular the women, lacked the security of their contemporaries who could inherit the family home from their relations. Space within Deir el-Medina was strictly limited and there was no room for private property within the mud-brick walls, and no possibility of building the random extensions that led to the organic growth of more typical Egyptian villages. There was a real danger that the death of the breadwinner, if he had no son to follow immediately in his footsteps, would lead to eviction from the home and village where the family had lived for generations. Not surprisingly, fathers pulled whatever strings they could to ensure that their sons followed them into the workforce. One ostracon even preserves an attempt at bribery as a father offers the scribe and two foremen generous presents so 'they might promote my boy'.[9] Although promotion technically lay in the hands of the vizier, it seems that he would act upon the advice of his officials.

An underlying feeling of financial insecurity may explain why so many of the workmen, and their womenfolk, were eager to acquire private wealth by whatever means they could. We find the villagers exploiting their special skills labouring for others, developing a brisk trade in coffins and stelae, trading their surplus government rations and raising crops and small animals for barter. The Deir el-Medina family tombs demonstrate that many of the villagers were relatively affluent. This free enterprise was to make it hard for the authorities to use sudden, unexplained wealth as evidence of crime – the accused could simply argue that they had been exploiting their own resources. Thus, in one papyrus, a woman is able to explain away her employment of slaves: 'I bought them in exchange for garden produce.'[10]

Life at Deir el-Medina followed a predictable pattern. Every ten days the workmen would kiss their families goodbye and leave the village, walking the short distance into the Valley. Here they would spend the next eight days working in the tombs and the nights sleeping in temporary huts, before returning home to Deir el-Medina for the ninth and tenth days – their weekend. Those left behind in the village led a confined, slightly claustrophobic existence unlike life anywhere else in the Nile Valley. With security of paramount importance, Deir el-Medina was surrounded by a thick mud-brick wall which effectively separated the villagers from the outside world. For many years there was only one gateway; the single entrance allowed security guards employed by the vizier to examine and if necessary search anyone wishing to enter or leave the village. When expansion necessitated the provision of a second gateway, this policy of strict control was maintained.

Within the wall, the identical terraced houses stretched in prim, dark, ordered lines with none of the untidiness or haphazard growth that characterised other Egyptian villages. Beyond the wall there were tombs, chapels and desert; the cultivated land petered out some half a mile away, while the River Nile flowed a further two miles to the south. The other west bank settlements were a good walk away. In many ways the authorities regarded this isolation as a good thing: isolation equalled security for the royal tombs. There was, however, one major drawback. With no natural water supply the villagers were entirely dependent upon the vizier's office for their rations of water, food, clothing and consumables.

The New Kingdom monarchs were pleased with their security arrangements. The inconspicuous entrances to the tombs were well guarded, entrance to and exit from the necropolis was strictly controlled, the workmen were isolated and kept under constant supervision, and a top-secret master-plan allowed frequent tours of inspection designed to detect even the most minor breaches of tomb security. Although the late Eighteenth Dynasty had seen an unfortunate spate of thefts from the royal tombs, with the burials of Tuthmosis IV, Amenhotep III and Tutankhamen all suffering some damage, Horemheb had put an end to west bank lawlessness by implementing a thorough revision of necropolis administration plus a security clamp-down at Deir el-Medina.

So confident were the royal architects – or did they perhaps realise that everyone already knew the location of the tombs? – that the Nineteenth and Twentieth Dynasty monarchs abandoned the practice of concealing the tomb doorways, choosing instead to make a feature of the entrance, which now presented an imposing façade to the world. The tomb of Ramesses II (KV 7), for example, was protected by a simple wooden door the bolts and seals of which would not have posed a challenge to anyone wishing to enter. With security totally dependent upon the necropolis guards, the stone lintel above the doorway was decorated with the image of the sun positioned between the goddesses Isis and Nephthys, while the inner faces of the pillars showed Maat kneeling above the lily and papyrus plants that symbolise Upper and Lower Egypt.

# CHAPTER 9

# THE ROBBERS OF
# THE WEST BANK

As regal authority weakened at the end of the Nineteenth Dynasty the workmen of Deir el-Medina experienced official neglect and the Theban monuments started to come under attack. Papyrus Salt 124 (BM 10055) highlights a spectacular instance of lawlessness in the royal necropolis. The chief workman Paneb has actually been caught stealing from the tomb of Seti II:

> And when the burial of all the kings was made I reported Paneb's theft of the things of King Seti Merenptah . . . and he took away the covering of his chariot . . . and he took away his wines and sat on the sarcophagus of Pharaoh although he was buried . . . and he hacked up the ground which is sealed in the place which is hidden. And yet he swore the oath saying, 'I did not upset a stone in the neighbourhood of the Place of Pharaoh.'[1]

Paneb is the all-round bad guy whom we first met bribing the vizier in Chapter 2. He now stands accused of a whole series of offences including theft, assault, and attempted murder. We shall hear of him again.

The authorities were only too well aware that security in the necropolis was to a large extent dependent upon the goodwill of the Deir el-Medina residents. As far as possible, the workmen were to be kept happy, their somewhat strident demands met with tact and courtesy. Thus, even during the affluent reign of Ramesses II, we find the mayor of western Thebes writing to reassure his workforce:

> The mayor of western Thebes, Ramose, greets the chief workmen and the whole gang ... Look, the governor and vizier Paser has sent to me saying, 'Let the dues be brought for the workmen of the Royal Tomb, namely vegetables, fish, firewood, jars of beer, food and milk. Do not let a scrap of it remain outstanding ... Do not let me find that you have held anything that is due back as balance. Be careful over this.'[2]

In times of civil unrest or shortage the need to provision Deir el-Medina could pose an acute administrative headache. The workmen were an argumentative lot, prone to down tools at the slightest provocation. Their specialised knowledge seems to have allowed them a freedom that other, less privileged workers may well have envied, and complaints from the 'Servants in the Place of Truth' bypassed the usual administrative channels and went straight to the top:

> the crew having gone out, being hungry, said, 'We have gone out because we are hungry; there is no wood, no vegetables, no fish ... We came to ask the advice of the magistrates of the tribunal and they stated, "The people of the tomb are in the right."'[3]

The Twentieth Dynasty ostracon quoted above dates to the impoverished reign of Ramesses III. Government officials have been sent to the west bank to negotiate with the workers who have ceased work in protest at the non-delivery of rations. It compares closely with the Turin Strike Papyrus, which details further discontent amongst the workers in Year 29 of Ramesses III and includes a mention of thefts from the tombs of Ramesses II and his sons (KV 5):

> Now Userhat and Patwere have stripped stones from above the tomb of Osiris King Usermaatre Setepenre [Ramesses II] ... and Kenena son of Ruta did it in the same manner above the tomb of the royal children of King Usermaatre Setepenre.[4]

Clearly, Egypt's faltering economy was starting to affect her workforce, who were suffering the effects of high inflation. Petty crimes, the stripping of precious metals from the walls of the temples or the pilfering of the temple stores, were now almost everyday occurrences. It was not until the late Twentieth Dynasty, however, that the royal tombs came under serious threat. Kings Ramesses IV–XI, a confusing succession of fathers, sons, and brothers, were fated to rule over a land increasingly suffering the interconnected effects of African drought, low Nile levels, bad harvests, famine, inflation, official corruption and civil unrest. These, of course, represent the classic background for temple- and tomb-robbery.

Preserved from this unstable time is an assortment of late Ramesside judicial records which are today collectively known as the 'Tomb-Robbery Papyri'. These records, which include lists of suspects, inventories of stolen goods and reports of temple and tomb inspections, provide us with the details of just some of the crimes committed and solved in the royal necropolis and its immediate environs during the reigns of Ramesses IX and Ramesses XI. One of the earliest, Papyrus Meyer B, tells of the theft of equipment and textiles from the tomb of Ramesses VI (KV 9):

> The foreigner Nesamen took us up and showed us the tomb

of King Nebmaatre-Meryamen [Ramesses VI] ... and I spent four days breaking into it, we all five being present. We opened up the tomb and entered it ... We found ... of bronze, a bronze cauldron, three bronze bowls, a ewer ... We weighed out the copper of the objects and the vessels and found it to be 500 *deben*, 100 *deben* being the share of each man. We opened two chests full of clothes ... We found a basket of clothes lying there, we opened it and found twenty-five shawls of coloured cloth.[5]

The robbers, whose numbers had at one stage included 'the youngster of the tomb', presumably a necropolis workman, were able to effect an inconspicuous entrance by burrowing from an adjacent earlier tomb. The metals and textiles thus seized were destined to re-enter the economy either as household items or as exchange goods.

Metal was particularly useful: easily recycled and very difficult to trace, it could be hoarded, bartered or used as payment for services rendered. It also made a useful bribe. Here, in a document dating to the reign of Ramesses XI, the gardener Kar tells of three illicit expeditions to strip the gold foil from the door-jambs of the Ramesseum. Once again, the thieves are those who might have been expected to guard the treasures of the late king:

We paid another visit to the door-jambs together with the priest Hori, son of Pakharu, the scribe of the temple, Sedi, and the priest Nesamen ... We took away five *kite* of gold and used it to buy barley in Thebes, and split it between ourselves. Now some days later, the scribe of the temple, Sedi, came again bringing three men with him. They went again to the door-jambs and brought away four *kite* of gold. We divided it among ourselves and him. Now after some days our supervisor, Peminu, argued with us saying, 'You have given me nothing.' So we went back to the door-jambs and brought five *kite* of gold from them, and exchanged it for an ox which we gave to Peminu. Now the scribe of the royal archives, Sutekhmose, heard whisper of what we had done, and he threatened us saying, 'I am going to report it to the high priest of Amen.' So we took away three *kite* of gold and gave them to the scribe of the royal archives.[6]

Five *kite* of gold, here the value of an ox, was the equivalent of 60 *deben* of copper. The fence who swapped his ox for the gold must have realised that he was handling stolen goods; under normal circumstances private individuals would not have had access to such large quantities of precious metal. Presumably he adjusted his price accordingly. Those who grew suddenly and inexplicably affluent were likely to attract the attention of the authorities, although the tradition of bartering home-grown produce made such suspicions difficult to prove.

Papyrus Leopold II – Amherst preserves the detailed confession of the stonemason and habitual thief Amenpanufer who, called to account before the Year 16 court of Ramesses IX, admits to stealing from the tomb of the Seventeenth Dynasty king Sobekemsaf II and, almost as an aside, to the bribery of the local bureaucrats. The burning of the coffins mentioned in the statement was no mindless act of vandalism, but a time-honoured means of separating the gold leaf from the wood.

We went to rob the tombs as is our usual habit, and we found the pyramid tomb of King Sobekemsaf, this tomb being unlike the pyramids and tombs of the nobles which we usually rob. We took our copper tools and forced a way into the pyramid of this king through its innermost part. We located the underground chambers and, taking lighted candles in our hands, went down ... [We] found the god lying at the back of his burial place. And we found the burial place of Queen Nubkhaas, his consort, beside him, it being

protected and guarded by plaster and covered with rubble
... We opened their sarcophagi and their coffins, and found
the noble mummy of the king equipped with a sword. There
were a large number of amulets and jewels of gold on his
neck, and he wore a headpiece of gold. The noble mummy of
the king was completely covered in gold and his coffins were
decorated with gold and with silver inside and out, and
inlaid with various precious stones. We collected the gold
that we found on the mummy of the god including the
amulets and jewels which were on his neck ... We set fire to
their coffins ...

After some days the district officers of Thebes heard that
we had been robbing in the west, and they arrested me and
imprisoned me in the office of the mayor of Thebes. I took
the twenty *deben* of gold that represented my share and I
gave them to Khaemope, the district scribe of the landing
quay of Thebes. He released me and I rejoined my colleagues
and they compensated me with a share again. And so I got
into the habit of robbing the tombs.[7]

We are told that the gang, betrayed by the loquacious Amenpanufer, were first examined 'by beating with sticks and their feet and
hands were [? – either beaten or twisted]', and then taken over to
the west bank where they were required to identify the violated
tomb. They were then returned to prison, to await the judgement
of Pharaoh.

The Tomb-Robbery Papyri confirm that many of the thefts were
committed by west bank residents, principally those living in Deir
el-Medina and in Maiunehes, a town close by the Medinet Habu
mortuary temple of Ramesses III. The citizens of eastern Thebes
were by no means averse to plundering the temples and tombs,
but the Nile posed an effective deterrent to casual looting. Some
determined thieves persevered, either using their own boats or
hiring vessels to ferry both themselves and their ill-gotten gains

across the river. The boatman, neither a full nor a well-paid member of the gang, was often the weak link in the chain of secrecy, one which the authorities were quick to follow up:

> We entered the tombs of the west of Thebes and we stripped off the silver and the gold ... We went all six of us together, and the fisherman Panekhemope ferried us over to the west and his share was exactly the same as mine.[8]

In a contemporary papyrus Panekhemope the ferryman explains his actions:

> I ferried them over by night, and landed them on the west bank of Thebes. They said to me, 'wait until we return.' Now on the evening of the next day they returned and called to me in the night, and I went to them on the bank. I took all six of them and brought them to this side of the river and landed them at Thebes. And after some days Panekhtresi came to bring me three *kite* of gold.[9]

These robberies were not the simple, opportunistic crimes that we might suppose. The gangs were both well-organised and well-informed, and they often had the tacit backing of the officials responsible for guarding the tombs. The state bureaucracy was by now irredeemably infected with corruption which allowed even the highest ranking Theban officials to profit from organised crime. As we have seen in the Leopold II–Amherst Papyrus, many would, for a consideration, look the other way. Papyrus Abbott, a fascinating document covering just four days in Year 16 of Ramesses IX, goes further in pointing the finger of suspicion firmly at one Paweraa, master-criminal and mayor of Thebes.

Paweraa, as mayor of western Thebes and chief of the necropolis police, had ultimate control over west bank security. Unfortunately, he was not a man of good character, and Paser, the parallel mayor of eastern Thebes, had grown increasingly suspicious of his colleague. An investigation instigated by Paser had led to the Year 16 trial of those responsible for the desecration of the tomb of Sobekemsaf II which has been quoted above. Now this was to be followed by a government inspection of the necropolis, under the chairmanship of the vizier and city-governor Khaemwaset. Khaemwaset, a friend of Paweraa, drew the surprising conclusion that there was no cause for concern. Of the ten royal tombs examined, only one, that of Sobekemsaf II, had been violated, although two others betrayed the unmistakable signs of an attempted break-in. The tombs of the nobles were a different matter, but no one was particularly concerned about the non-royal burials:

> The tombs and burial chambers in which the blessed ones of old, the male and female citizens, rest on the west of Thebes; it was found that thieves had plundered them all, dragging the owners from their inner and outer coffins and leaving them in the desert. The funeral outfits which had been given to them were stolen, together with the gold and silver and fittings which ornamented their inner coffins.[10]

It was official. The necropolis was secure, Paweraa was publicly vindicated and Paser was enraged as a triumphal band of police, security guards and necropolis workmen paraded in front of his house. He vowed at once to write to Pharaoh, passing on secret information obtained from two honest necropolis scribes. Paweraa responded by filing a complaint against Paser; it had been a blatant breach of procedure, he alleged, for the scribes to report to the mayor of eastern Thebes when they should have gone straight to the vizier. The next day the court sat, considered the evidence, and threw Paser's case out. A report to this effect was duly filed in the vizier's archive. Undaunted, Paser persevered, made a further application, and appeared to win his case. Just as it seems that

Paweraa was to be brought to justice, however, the textual sources end. While Paweraa continues to flourish, both Paser and Khaemwaset disappear from the record, never to be heard of again. Needless to say, the tomb-robberies continue as before.

Once a crime had been detected and reported to the vizier's office, the wheels of justice creaked into operation. Those suspected of involvement were arrested, taken across the river and interrogated. The vizier himself might then travel to the west bank to test the truth of the witness statement at the scene of the crime. Next the suspect would appear before the Theban court where the evidence would be considered by a panel of high-ranking judges including the vizier. Those found guilty would be referred to Pharaoh for the ultimate sanction to be applied. The punishments that this court handed out during the reign of Ramesses IX were apparently so severe that when, some thirty years later during Year 19 of Ramesses XI, the witness Tjauenany was interrogated on suspicion of robbing the necropolis, the memory of the earlier deaths was still vivid in his mind:

'If I speak untruthfully, may I be mutilated and sent to Kush.'

The vizier said to him: 'What is the story behind your going to the great tombs?'

He said: 'I saw the punishment that was inflicted upon the thieves in the time of the vizier Khaemwaset. Is it likely, then, that I would risk incurring such a death?'

He was again examined with the stick on his feet and hands.

He said: 'I saw nothing and I did nothing myself.'

The vizier spoke to him: 'Look, you have already been beaten, but if someone else comes and accuses you I will take further action.'

He said: 'If someone else comes and accuses me you can inflict any manner of terrible punishment on me!'

He was examined again with the stick, the birch and [twisting].[11]

A reluctant witness could usually be persuaded to talk:

> The herdsman Bukhaaf. He said, 'it was Pewer, a workman of the necropolis, who showed us the tomb of Queen Hebrezet.' They said to him, 'The tomb that you entered, in what state did you find it?' He said, 'I found it open.' He was examined with the aid of a stick again. He said, 'Leave me alone, I will tell.'[12]

However, there was always the danger that an overenthusiastic beating might persuade a witness to confess to a crime he had not committed. This happened in the case of the coppersmith Paikhure who claimed to have robbed the tomb of Queen Isis shortly before the tomb of Sobekemsaf II was violated. When the coppersmith, blindfolded and closely guarded, was taken to the tombs and the blindfold removed, he was unable to identify the appropriate tomb, indicating instead an empty tomb and a workman's hut:

> The officials had this coppersmith subjected to a particularly severe examination in the Great Valley, but it could not be determined that he knew of any place there except for the two places that he had pointed out. He swore the oath of the king on pain of being beaten, of having his nose and ears cut off, and of being impaled, saying, 'I know of no place here among the tombs except this tomb which is open and this hut which I pointed out to you.'[13]

It appears in this case that Paikhure was a false witness, set up by the devious Paweraa in order to discredit the honest Paser's evidence. The tomb of Isis had indeed been robbed; whether this was done by Paikhure or some other we shall never know.

Occasionally even the most severe of beatings failed to persuade the witness. The same papyrus records the case of Amenkhau, a temple musician, who has been falsely accused of participating in a robbery by his enemy Perpethew. Amenkhau explains his position to the court: 'I said to him, "You'll be put to death for your crime." He said to me, "If I am, I will take you with me!"' As Amenkhau stuck to his story while enduring a severe flogging, he was eventually released.

The reign of Ramesses XI saw Pharaoh confined to the north of Egypt, with virtual civil war at Thebes. Most of the royal tombs now stood empty and exposed, while the mortuary temples of Ramesses II and III had been vandalised. So insecure was the Theban west bank that Ramesses XI abandoned his own almost complete tomb in the Valley of the Kings (KV 4), making alternative plans to be buried in the north. This did little to boost morale among the necropolis workforce, and the crime rate rose alarmingly. Eventually, at the end of the Twentieth Dynasty, Deir el-Medina was abandoned and its workforce resettled at Medinet Habu. Here, deprived of their principal trade, the villagers soon became absorbed into the general Theban population.

With the death of Ramesses XI came the end of the New Kingdom. Egypt was now split in two with Smendes, founder of the Third Intermediate Period Twenty-first Dynasty, ruling in the north, while the High Priests of Amen gradually brought the south under control. Three letters, dating to the time of the High Priest Herihor and all dealing with the same subject, confirm that Thebes was still unstable:

The General of Pharaoh to the scribe of the necropolis Zaroi. I have noted all the matters that you wrote about. Now, as to the matter of the two Medjay, whom you said spoke of my affairs . . . have these two Medjay brought to this house, and let them put a stop to their words altogether. If they perceive that it is true, let them put them in two sacks and throw them into the river by night, without anyone in the land knowing about it.[14]

Clearly the two Medjay, who know more than they should about some criminal matter, have broken their silence. They are now to pay a heavy price for their indiscretion.

The new southern rulers turned their attention to the ravaged west bank. A scene of utter confusion met their eyes. The plundered tombs of the Pharaohs were open to the world, the discarded bodies of the kings in a disgraceful condition. Clearly a new strategy was needed. If the necropolis guards could not beat the thieves, why not join them? If the promise of hidden gold was attracting the thieves to the tombs, the well-publicised removal of the gold would surely remove all temptation, allowing the mummies to rest in peace and the royal spirits to enjoy eternal life. As an added bonus, the valuables collected from the royal tombs could then be used to swell the sadly-depleted state coffers.

The priests set to work. All known royal tombs were opened and emptied and their mummies transferred to temporary workshops. Here they were stripped, re-bandaged, labelled and placed in plain wooden coffins. The newly impoverished mummies were then stored in convenient, well-guarded chambers dotted about the necropolis. From time to time these collections were inspected and moved, until eventually there was a major collection of royal mummies housed in the tomb of the High Priest Pinodjem II at Deir el-Bahari (DB 320) and a second royal cache stored in the tomb of Amenhotep II (KV 35). Here the once magnificent kings and queens of Egypt, bereft of their golden treasures, waited patiently as the centuries passed. The Deir el-Bahari cache was to be rediscovered in 1881, the Amenhotep II cache in 1898.

Meanwhile, in the north, the royal family in their enforced

isolation from the Valley of the Kings had also developed a new strategy. From this time onwards, their burials were to be included within the precincts of the temples where they could be guarded by the temple priests. The nobles would have to provide for their own burials, and their once-elaborate tombs now evolved into more discreet family vaults. This new system was to prove highly effective. The royal tombs of Tanis, although plundered during the Ptolemaic age, still contained a substantial amount of funerary equipment when rediscovered during the Second World War. These treasures, including gold jewellery, gold and silver vessels, shabti figures and the spectacular silver coffins of Psusennes and Shoshenk-Hekakheperre, are now housed in Cairo Museum. The tombs of the Twenty-sixth Dynasty kings at Sais have never been found, although Herodotus preserves their memory:

> The Saites buried within the temple precincts all kings who were natives of their province, and so it even contains the tomb of Amasis as well as that of Apries and his family. The tomb of the former is farther from the sanctuary than the tomb of the latter, yet it is also within the temple. It is a great colonnade of stone, richly adorned, the pillars of which are carved in the form of palm trees. In this colonnade is a chamber with folding doors and the place where the coffin lies is behind these doors.[15]

# CHAPTER 10

# THE VILLAGER AND
# THE ORACLE

Perhaps because of their enforced proximity and their isolation from the rest of the Theban population, or maybe as a reaction against the boring routine of their daily lives, the fifty or so families of Deir el-Medina were a remarkably quarrelsome and surprisingly light-fingered lot. At Deir el-Medina it seems that there was no notion of privacy. Everybody knew everybody else's business and the various households were both economically and emotionally interlinked. They supported, traded with, fought with, victimised and stole from each other depending on temperament.

Fortunately for the modern observer, the villagers were also an exceptionally literate group of people who committed even the most trivial of legal matters to writing, using limestone flakes and discarded potsherds as their journals. The fact that these records were kept for years, and were quoted in subsequent legal cases, serves to highlight the extent to which Egypt's legal system relied on legal precedent. Reading these documents, with their catalogue of petty misdemeanours setting neighbour against neighbour, it can be hard to remember that their authors were the élite of Egypt's workforce. The Servants in the Place of Truth were well paid and well respected and, certainly at times of firm state control, had no real need to resort to crime. When Deir el-Medina was abandoned at the end of the Twentieth Dynasty its virtually indestructible ostraca were left behind. These, together with the batch of surviving papyri which represent the remains of the legal archives, allow us to review the legal goings-on at Deir el-Medina in a way that is impossible for other dynastic communities.[1]

As we have already seen, official investigations into necropolis affairs were grave matters indeed, with those found guilty of offences against the state facing the harshest of punishments: banishment, mutilation, or death by impaling. Serious crimes were, however, the exception rather than the rule. Far more usual were the day-to-day internal disputes which we might expect to encounter in any closely confined group of people. Breaches of contract, often the failure to return borrowed or hired property, were common enough complaints, and arguments over borrowed donkeys seem to have occurred on an almost daily basis. Petty thieving, usually involving the loss of food and clothing, seems to have been a constant underlying theme of village life. Fortunately, if proximity fuelled the jealousy that prompted such crimes, it also helped in the detection of the offenders as no one could keep new-found wealth hidden for long. Property and inheritance disputes, too, occurred with surprising regularity. At Deir el-Medina, where so much was owned by the state, it was very important that the precise ownership of non-government property was clearly understood by all. All these matters were doubtless of the utmost importance to those involved, but they were of little interest to anyone outside the village. As such, they might properly be settled within the immediate community without any reference to the vizier's court at Thebes.

Just occasionally, matters were serious enough to attract the attention of the outside authorities who had ultimate responsibility for maintaining public order. During Year 6 of Ramesses IV we learn of the organisation of a gang of thieves, led by Sunero and Penmennefer, who stole from the village houses and hid their loot in the grounds of the Ramesseum. So heartless were these villains that included in the list of victims was Penmennefer's own father! We know that the gang were caught and called to account;

unfortunately, we do not know which court was involved, but it is likely that sooner or later the case would have been referred to the vizier's court at Thebes, where the offenders could receive a suitably serious punishment.[2]

Some disputes were so trivial that they never made it to court. Foremen, police chiefs, scribes and, indeed, anyone of known good character had the authority to act as arbitrator and settle differences in an informal but legally binding manner. Although admirably simple in its design, a major flaw in this legal option was the fact that the disgruntled loser, unwilling to accept the judgement, had the right to apply for the case to be reheard time and time again until he or she was eventually satisfied with the verdict. This flaw, unfortunately, also applied to the more formal court, or *kenbet*, so that some Deir el-Medina cases took years and even decades to reach any resolution. In Chapter 3 we met the police chief Mentmose who blatantly ignored the rulings of the court and took a startling eighteen years to pay for his pot of fat; this, as far as we can judge from the surviving records, was by no means unusual. Even when a verdict had been given and compensation specified, it seems that the court had little if any power to ensure that the judgement was fulfilled, so that it was often moral pressure from the rest of the community that caused the offender to put right a wrong.

The *kenbet* took the form of an open air tribunal whose members, temporarily accorded the title of 'officers of the court', were drawn from both the Deir el-Medina community and the government officials charged with the correct functioning of the village; a typical court might include the captains of the gang, the chief of the Medjay, the scribes of the vizier and a selection of prominent villagers. Given this local composition, the members of the tribunal were likely both to know the characters of the witnesses who appeared before them and to have useful background knowledge concerning their disputes. Far from biasing their judgement, it seems that this local knowledge was considered essential in helping them to reach the correct ruling.

The *kenbet* did not itself launch investigations. Rather, the court was convened as and when there were problems brought to its attention. The procedure was simple. The claimant would present his or her case, if possible naming witnesses and citing evidence, and would then be questioned by the tribunal. Next, the accused was entitled to speak, and he or she might also be subjected to questioning. In a more complicated case the court might then decide to summon further witnesses, or might even condescend to conduct its own mini-investigation. Once judgement had been pronounced – 'X is right, Y is wrong' – the loser might be forced to swear to right his or her wrong with appropriate compensation.

Very occasionally the *kenbet* might become involved in a criminal case. We know, for example, of the trial of the lady Kheria, initially accused of stealing a chisel belonging to a neighbour (a civil offence). Things went badly for Kheria when a search revealed a temple censer, property of the god Amen, hidden in her house. Found guilty of stealing from the temple (a criminal offence), and publicly denounced as 'a great false one, worthy of death', the details were forwarded to the vizier's office. Presumably a criminal trial at Thebes, and suitable punishment, 'so that no other woman at all shall again do likewise', would follow. This would, however, appear to have been an unusual case and it was rare for the *kenbet* and the vizier's court to overlap.

An appearance before the *kenbet* required the plaintiff to name a defendant. In a legal wrangle over a contract, an inheritance or property rights this would not pose a problem as the disputing parties would be obvious to everyone. In a case of civil misdemeanour such as theft or vandalism, however, this could be a considerable difficulty. Where there was no obvious culprit, where there was a suspect but neither evidence nor witnesses, or where the victim was unwilling to make a public accusation, there could be no trial.

Legal records show that cases involving a poor villager suing a rich one are rare. In many ways this is what we would expect to find: it is generally the poor who owe to the rich. However, we should not ignore the possibility that this is the unfortunate result of a legal system where the socially inferior might hesitate publicly to accuse a superior, and where the rich and powerful may have been able to exert undue influence over a jury composed primarily of villagers. The most frequently encountered legal cases are those where social equals dispute with each other. Cases involving a rich person suing a poor one are relatively infrequent, and it would appear that the powerful were often able to take matters into their own hands, resolving disputes informally, away from court.

In cases where the claimant was unwilling or unable to accuse a defendant an application to the local oracle provided an alternative legal route which was virtually guaranteed to give satisfaction. While the court carried a high burden of proof, the equivalent of 'beyond reasonable doubt', the omnipotent oracle needed absolutely no evidence at all. A question as vague as 'Has a member of the work-gang stolen them?' would receive the correct response.

Religion, or superstition, played an important part in village life. The villagers, lacking any scientific understanding of the world around them, were constantly seeking explanations for, and protection against, the otherwise inexplicable. Childbirth, for example, often a matter of life and death for both mother and baby, developed its own magical rituals as a direct response to the lack of medical knowledge. Although the demi-gods associated with pregnancy, Taweret and Bes, were bit-part players in the official state pantheon, they had an important role in private, domestic religion.

At a more general level, prayers offered to the gods, both national and local, were designed to influence the divinity to look favourably upon the plaintiff, and often took the form of a bribe – 'If I offer you bread and beer, will you look after me?' Those unfortunates stricken by sudden misfortune could be sure that they were experiencing retribution for a crime or crimes, whether committed knowingly or not. Blindness, common enough in the harsh glare and ever-present dust of the Egyptian desert, was a certain sign of divine displeasure, as the draughtsman Neferabu found out:

> I am a man who swore falsely by Ptah, Lord of *maat*. In consequence he made me see darkness in the daylight. Now I will proclaim his might to both the foolish and the wise, to the small and the great. Beware Ptah, Lord of *maat*! For he does not ignore anyone's deed. Refrain from uttering his name falsely. Behold! He that utters his name falsely, he will fall.[3]

More serious offences might be punished with death, the crocodile and the dog being two favoured means of execution in myth and legend. The New Kingdom *Tale of the Doomed Prince*, or *The Prince who was Threatened by Three Fates*, an ancient combination of the more modern *Sleeping Beauty* and *Rapunzel*, tells of the fates that haunt a young prince who has, so far as we can tell, done nothing to arouse the enmity of the gods.[4]

> Once upon a time there was a king who had everything his heart desired except a son. The king pleaded with the gods, and in due time his prayer was answered and his wife gave birth to a fine baby boy. Then the Hathors came to announce the boy's fate: 'He will die by the crocodile, the snake or the dog.' When the king heard this he was very much afraid. Seeking to protect his young son he had a house of stone built in the desert. Here the young prince could be kept indoors, away from danger.
> One day the lonely prince asked for a puppy and his father, unable to deny his son anything, gave him one. The boy and the dog were soon inseparable. When he became a

man the prince decided that he could no longer live in hiding. He would leave his home and challenge his fates. The prince and his dog drove off in a chariot and crossed the desert to the land of Nahrin. Here there was a beautiful princess imprisoned in a tower. Her father had decreed that she was to marry the man who could leap up to her window. The Egyptian prince joined the jumping suitors and was able to leap right up and kiss the princess. The king of Nahrin reluctantly gave permission for his beloved daughter to marry the unknown foreigner, and the couple settled down to married life.

The prince told his bride about his three fates. She demanded that he kill his faithful dog but he refused to betray his friend. The wife, respecting his loyalty, determined to protect her husband. Meanwhile, one of the three fates, the crocodile, had followed the prince from Egypt and was now settled in a nearby lake where it fought every day with a local spirit.

One night a snake came to kill the prince as he slept. His wife was watching over him and she gave the snake a bowl of wine to drink. She then hacked the sleepy serpent to pieces and woke her husband to show him what she had done. Another day the prince was out walking when his dog spoke to him, 'I am your fate!' In terror the prince ran away and jumped in the lake, whereupon the crocodile seized him. The crocodile spoke, 'I am your fate, but if you help me to fight the spirit I will release you.'

Unfortunately, the remainder of the tale is missing. However, enough is preserved to suggest that there was a happy ending and that the young prince lived happily ever after.

The oracle was the one method by which the ordinary Egyptian could communicate directly with a divine being without using Pharaoh as an intermediary. A consultation allowed the supplicant to question the god in person and, in contrast to one who merely prayed, he or she would receive a reply which the villagers would accept as legally binding. The tradition of the ordinary Egyptian consulting the oracle is one that, although perhaps started as early as the Old Kingdom, really developed during the New Kingdom as religious processions became increasingly popular. Now the images of the gods started to leave the dark privacy of the sanctuary hidden deep within the temple. Embarking on a boat, concealed within a portable shrine, they were carried through the streets of Egypt's towns and cities, allowing the people a fleeting contact with their gods.[5] As the bearers rested at certain predetermined points, the people were able to approach the god and ask his or her advice. By the end of the New Kingdom, when the bureaucracy appeared irredeemably corrupt, the oracle was perhaps seen as the more impartial, and certainly cheaper, arbitrator; there is no record of anyone caught attempting to bribe the oracle, and it is perhaps less likely that the oracle would be swayed by the wealth or social standing of the accused.

The kings of Egypt were at liberty to consult the highest ranking of the state gods. When Queen Hatchepsut wished to confirm her right to rule Egypt, she sought guidance from Amen-Re himself:

> . . . very great oracle in the presence of this good god, proclaiming for me the kingship of the Two Lands, Upper and Lower Egypt . . . Being the ordination of the Two Lands for me in the South Hall of Luxor, while His Majesty [Amen] delivered an oracle in the presence of this good god.[6]

Similarly Tuthmosis III had his right to rule confirmed by Amen. Ramesses II, needing to appoint a new High Priest of Amen, read out the list of suitable applicants and allowed the god to make his choice. Curiously, we find that the wishes of the gods often coincided with the wishes of the kings!

Members of the élite, priests and bureaucrats, were important enough to be granted an audience with their local patron deity. Ptah gave advice at Memphis; Amen, Mut, Khonsu and Montu at Karnak; and so on. More humble persons did not trouble the state gods; they were expected to consult their own specific local deity who, presumably, would have a better knowledge of local affairs. At Deir el-Medina this was the deified King Amenhotep I, long considered to be the founder of the necropolis work-gangs, and possibly the first monarch to be buried in the new royal cemetery. At least six subtly different versions of Amenhotep were worshipped at Deir el-Medina – Amenhotep of the Village, Amenhotep of the Forecourt and Amenhotep of the Garden being just three.

Amenhotep, both king and god, made an eminently suitable oracle because his pronouncements had both legal and divine authority. He was a versatile judge, happy to pronounce on matters as diverse as property ownership, business deals, affairs of the heart and matters of health. He could look into the past to solve mysteries, could provide a valuation for a coffin or a statue, and could see into the future to prophesy the unknown. He could even state whether an unborn child would live or die.

His speciality, however, the area where he triumphed over the court, was in answering questions that were not merely points of law. Thus he could identify thieves and settle the matters of inheritance and landed property that so vexed the villagers. When Kenna restored a ruined house, only to have Merysekhmet claim an interest in the property, Amenhotep, on procession through the necropolis, gave his judgement outside the tomb of Kaha (TT 360). The house did indeed belong to Kenna and he had no need to share it.

Understandably, those who wrote of the work of the oracle were more interested in preserving the judgements than describing the mechanics of an operation with which, it was assumed, everyone was already familiar. This leaves us lacking many essential details in our reconstruction of an oracular consultation, which is, through necessity, drawn from a combination of randomly preserved judgements plus a detailed scene in the Theban tomb of the priest Amenmose (TT 19).[7]

In Amenmose's tomb is depicted Amenhotep of the Forecourt as he leaves his temple. The king, or rather his statue, is not hidden by a portable shrine but is revealed to his people. He sits, bearing full regalia, on a splendid throne which is carried on a litter borne shoulder-high by four priests. Four others walk close by, waving fans and carrying flowers. The procession is a colourful, cheerful, noisy event; there are female musicians, men preparing offerings and two supplicants who walk with bowed heads, and an excited crowd of villagers may be imagined to be following behind. Along the ceremonial route the god would occasionally stop, presumably to allow his bearers to take a much-needed rest. Now the supplicants, who may have already put in a formal request to approach the oracle, would be given the opportunity to pose their problem.

The god would reply by moving – or causing his bearers to move – forwards (a positive response) or backwards (a negative response). We do not know what happened if the bearers felt compelled to move in different directions; would the god effectively stand still, and fail to provide an answer? Obviously, questions with a simple yes or no answer were the easiest for the god to deal with, but it was possible, with some ingenuity, to expand the possibilities. A list of names might be read out, for example, and the god would respond to that of the guilty party. Or different solutions to a particular problem might be written on separate ostraca; these could then be placed before the god who would move in the appropriate direction.

Some, when submitting a complicated matter involving property rights, prepared a complete legal case for the god. Others relied on supernatural assistance. The draughtsman Kaha, whose garments had been stolen by an unknown thief, employed a professional wise-man to read out a list of the houses in the village. This combination of local superstition and official religion paid off. When the house of the scribe Amennakht was mentioned, the god indicated that the garments were 'with his daughter'.

The case of Kaha is one of several instances in which we are told that the god himself spoke in judgement. It is difficult to see how sound effects could have been accomplished without very obvious trickery (assuming, of course, that the statue did not actually speak), and it seems likely that the writers who claim to have heard the god's words are merely exaggerating their accounts of the proceedings. However, even if we eliminate the possibility of the god speaking, we are still left with a major stumbling block to our understanding of the oracle: we have absolutely no idea how the statue came to move. We do know that the men who carried the god were lay-priests drawn from the workforce. Did their background knowledge enable them to vote with their feet, making the consultation essentially a form of trial by jury? Or was the process more subtle, with the bearers unconsciously employing their own knowledge while believing themselves to be moved by the god? It is even possible, but perhaps less likely, that the god did not move at all, but that his willing witnesses merely believed that he did.

Whatever the mechanics of the operation, one thing is clear. The verdicts almost always concurred with local opinion and the watching crowd were generally quick to support the oracle's judgement. This must have been an important factor in maintaining the credibility of the god. While we know that a court judgement would be followed by the pronouncement of a suitable penalty, the oracle ostraca tend to end with the verdict. We therefore do not know whether the oracle routinely suggested an appropriate punishment, or whether he left that to the watching villagers. Certainly, it was very hard to appeal against the oracle's public decision. Nevertheless, individuals did occasionally attempt to clear their name. When the scribe Wennefer accused Huy of stealing some lamps, and a search indeed revealed the said lamps in Huy's hut, the accused appealed to the oracle proclaiming his innocence. The oracle, however, was not convinced and Huy remained condemned.

In at least one case it would appear that the guilt of the accused was not proved beyond all reasonable doubt. Papyrus BM 10335 is a New Kingdom document which tells the tale of the unfortunate farmer Petjauemdiamen, accused of stealing five shirts from a local warehouse being guarded by the servant Amenemwia.[8] Amenem-wia, anxious to have the stolen property restored, had approached his local oracle, Amen of Pakhenty, and had read out a list of names. At the mention of Petjauemdiamen the god had moved – a clear sign of guilt. Petjauemdiamen, however, refused to accept the verdict and, turning his back on the god – 'I am in disgrace with my god; I will approach another' – he appealed to Amen of Tashenyt – in vain. He then applied to a third oracle, Amen-Bukentef, before returning to the first Amen, who once again declared him guilty of theft.

At this point Petjauemdiamen's hitherto loyal friends lost all patience and administered a sound thrashing which caused him to confess. Did his friends know, without having any actual proof, that the accused was truly a thief? Did he feel compelled to confess to get his ordeal over? We will never know. However, the case does leave lingering doubts in the mind of the reader – doubts which may also have been felt by the oracle, who ordered the victim Amenemwia to forgo the compensatory payment that normally would have been his right.

To modern eyes, the oracle system appears open to the most blatant abuse. The possibility that the oracle could be rigged had at least occurred to the Egyptians: 'Do not falsify the oracle on papyrus and so harm the plans of the god. Do not invent for yourself the power of a god as if there were no fate and no destiny.'[9] However, it seems reasonable to assume that any obvious manipulation of the system would not have escaped notice in a community as tight-knit as that of Deir el-Medina, where respect for the oracle lasted for centuries.

# Chapter 11

## Sex Crimes

The chief workman Paneb, whom we last encountered looting the tomb of Seti II in Chapter 9, had clearly been a busy boy. Among the additional charges levelled against him in Papyrus Salt 124 are:

> Charge concerning his robbing Iyemwaw of her garment and he threw her on top of the wall and [violated?] her ...
>
> Paneb slept with the citizeness Tuy, when she was the wife of the workman Kenna. He slept with the citizeness Huenro when she was with Pendua; he slept with the citizeness Huenro when she was with Hesysenebef. And after he had slept with Huenro he slept with Webkhet her daughter. And Apahte, his son, also slept with Webkhet.[1]

When allied with accusations of mistreating the necropolis workmen, embezzlement, drunken murderous outbursts and perverting the course of justice, this makes a formidable list of offences. Papyrus Salt would appear to be a draft copy of a letter of complaint addressed to the vizier. Unfortunately we do not know how the vizier reacted to the information disclosed. Paneb's fate goes unrecorded since he disappears from our view, but the then vizier Hori has gone on record as one who dealt harshly with offences against the state. Good luck has preserved a separate ostracon that records the divorce of Huenro and the cuckolded

Hesysenebef, and we know that the young Webkhet went on to become a respectable married lady.

It is possible, but due to the damaged wording not entirely certain, that the assault on the lady Iyemwaw should be classed as rape. This assault in any case includes the theft of a garment, and so makes a logical appearance on Paneb's charge-sheet. The other debaucheries would appear to be cases of adultery or seduction. There is no suggestion of force being used, or even that the ladies were unwilling, although it would appear that their menfolk were not happy with the situation and it may have been that the women, as the wives of Paneb's subordinates, felt unable to refuse his attentions. Webkhet, daughter of Huenro, is the only spinster to be seduced; we do not know how old she was when she received the attentions of Paneb and his son, but again there is no suggestion that she was forced to have sex at too young an age. The stress placed on her part in the debaucheries, however, does suggest that sleeping with both a mother and her daughter was considered in some way undesirable, maybe even incestuous.

Why has this list of moral outrages been appended to a list of criminal complaints submitted to the vizier? Would Hori really have been interested in such banal affairs? Adultery was not a crime against the state but a private matter, one that might occasionally be reported to a local magistrate or even to a local court, but that was far more likely to be dealt with by the individuals or families concerned. It would appear that Paneb's social activities are included here not as acts worthy of punishment but as a sure and certain sign of his bad character.

Paneb has committed a breach of trust, possibly using his influential position to charm the women of his workmen, and he is without doubt a man of low morals. The villagers of Deir el-Medina, an unusually close-knit community, were not happy with such scandalous behaviour. This interpretation is backed up by a second, unconnected, Deir el-Medina case dealing with the transportation of fats, which opens with the curious and irrelevant accusation 'You copulated with a married woman in the place of carrying torches'. It is also supported by the Turin Indictment Papyrus which, while concerned with priestly irregularities, includes the 'Memorandum about the copulation he did with Tabes, daughter of Shuy and wife of Ahauty'. Finally, some years later we find Paneb's son, Penanuqet, complaining about one Userhet whose crimes apparently included robbing a royal tomb, stealing an ox and 'he slept with three married women'.[2]

Many observers, from Herodotus through almost to the present day, have so far misinterpreted Egypt's seemingly casual acceptance of matters sexual as to suggest that dynastic society was essentially lacking in morals. This is not surprising. We all approach the past burdened with our own cultural conditioning; to the eminent Victorians who first published, and censored, works of Egyptian art and literature, making them accessible to a wide audience, the random appearance of what they considered to be pornography was shocking. Incest, polygamy, ithyphallic gods, transparent dresses, unchaperoned women, sensual love poetry, erotic papyri, the immoral (and Greek) Cleopatra and a complete absence of state and religious wedding rituals – all combined to suggest a society of sexual licence, a marked contrast to the strait-laced formal society (although not necessarily to the informal society) of the observers themselves.

Many of these myths of sexual licence evaporate on closer inspection. The image of a highly incestuous, polygamous society can be dismissed as an exaggeration. While neither was prohibited by law, both incest and polygamy were almost entirely royal prerogatives adopted for a specific purpose, and as such were rarely encountered outside the royal palace.[3] The inclusion of sexual references in religious rituals is harder for us to accept, conditioned as we are to think of religion as a 'pure' subject, divorced from matters of the flesh. The Egyptians saw things very differently. They, as farmers, understood that their lives were totally dependent upon the fertility of the Nile Valley. Their fields, their animals and, of course, their women all had a natural reproductive cycle which was essential for the continuance of Egypt and which should therefore be celebrated rather than denied.

It was entirely natural that fertility, in all its aspects, should play a part in Egyptian theology. Thus in one version of the creation myth we find the lone creator god creating the other gods single-handed, by masturbation. This, to the Egyptians, was logical rather than shocking, as was the fact that their gods exhibited the same desires as their human creators. An easy acceptance of the reproductive function did not, however, mean that the Egyptians were happy for their own partners to indulge in rampant, promiscuous sex.

Marriage was seen as a private matter, of concern only to the families involved. On her 'wedding day', the bride would simply leave the home of her parents and move into the home of her husband. With no state or civil wedding ceremony and no official register of marriage, cohabitation is often our only means of determining whether a couple considered themselves to be man and wife. In the past this caused historians a great deal of confusion. Today, as Western society grows accustomed to unmarried partners living together, we have a better understanding of how the system would have worked. One important thing is now evident: the confusion has been all in the minds of the observers. Couples, their families, friends and neighbours, had no trouble identifying who belonged with whom.

Sex between single consenting adults posed little problem to Egyptian society, and there was little or no stigma attached to illegitimate children. Once a couple were acknowledged to be married, however, they were expected to conform to the morals of their society. This meant that the wife was expected to remain faithful to her husband, who could then be sure that the children he was raising, and who were destined to inherit his property, were indeed his own. Unfortunately, fidelity could not always be guaranteed and only Pharaoh had the resources to keep his womenfolk safely tucked away. Most wives played a full and active role in community life and might fall prey to the charms of one such as Paneb.

It was, moreover, a popular male belief that married women were rapacious temptresses, eager to seduce innocent young men. Over the centuries the scribes evidently felt it necessary to warn their male readers of this danger:[4]

> If you want friendships to last in the house that you enter as a master, brother or friend, wherever you enter, beware of approaching the women! Unhappy is the place where this is done, unwelcome is he who intrudes.
>
> The Old Kingdom scribe Ptah-hotep

> Beware of the woman who is a stranger, who is not known in her town. Do not stare at her as she passes by and do not have intercourse with her. A woman who is away from her husband is a deep water whose course is unknown.
>
> The New Kingdom scribe Any

> He who makes love to a woman who has a husband will be killed on her doorstep ... Do not fornicate with a married woman. He who fornicates with a married woman on her bed, his wife will be copulated with on the ground [presumably rape is intended here].
>
> The Late Period scribe Ankhsheshonq

Here the perceived danger is not one of the pure young boy being tainted by proximity to immorality or vice, but a more practical concern that the wronged husband will seek to revenge himself on the discovered lover. As in many societies, it seems that the wronged husband's swift physical response in such a situation would have been considered legally justified.

There were many – Herodotus, for one – prepared to believe that the wives of Egypt were incorrigibly promiscuous:

> Following the death of King Sesostris his son Pheron mounted the throne. Pheron undertook no warlike expeditions, being struck with blindness ... At last, in the eleventh year of blindness, a pronouncement from the oracle of Buto reached him. The time of his punishment had expired and he should now recover his sight by washing his eyes with urine of a woman who had been faithful to her husband, and who had never preferred another man to him. The king turned first to his wife but to no purpose; he remained as blind as before. So then he experimented with other women until eventually he succeeded in recovering his sight. The king then assembled all the women, apart from the virtuous one, and bringing them to the city that now bears the name Red-Clay, he burned them all. But the woman who caused his cure, he married.[5]

Here, as in the Westcar Papyrus, burning sanctioned by the king acting on behalf of the wronged husband(s) is cited as a suitable punishment for female infidelity.

The unfaithful wife features heavily in the Nineteenth Dynasty *Tale of Two Brothers*. Her fate, at the hands of her husband, is equally grim, denying as it does her chance of life after death:[6]

> Anubis and Bata were two brothers. Anubis, the elder, had a house and a wife. His younger brother lived with him, and was treated as a son. Bata worked for his brother, tending the cattle, ploughing the fields and harvesting the grain. He was a fine, vigorous young man.
>
> One day the brothers were in the field. Anubis asked his

brother to return to the house to collect some seed. Bata went, and found his brother's wife dressing her hair. The wife watched the strong young man hoist the grain onto his shoulders, and was impressed with his strength. She desired him, and spoke, 'Come, let us spend an hour together. And afterwards I will make you some new clothes.'

Bata was shocked by this proposal. 'Look, I regard you as a mother and my brother as a father. What a terrible thing you have said. Do not mention this again and I will tell no one what has happened.' Bata then picked up his burden and returned to the field.

The woman, left alone in the house, grew frightened, imagining that Bata would tell his brother what had happened. She decided to tell her side of the story first. Taking her cosmetics, she made herself up to look as if she had been beaten. Then she lay down, pretending to be sick. When her husband returned she did not get up to greet him, and she did not light the lamp. The house was in darkness, and peering through the gloom Anubis found his wife vomiting. When Anubis questioned her, she accused Bata of attempted seduction: 'Your brother said, "Come let us sleep together for an hour," but I would not listen to him and he beat me so that I would not tell you.'

Anubis, believing this improbable tale, set out to kill his brother. Fortunately Bata was warned of his brother's anger, and he ran away. Eventually he was able to tell Anubis the true story, and Anubis returned home to kill his faithless wife, throwing her body to the dogs.

The only semi-official condemnation of fornication with married women comes from the negative confession which preceded admission to the afterlife in Chapter 125 of the *Book of the Dead*: 'I have not copulated with a married woman.' Adultery, then, would not appear to be illegal in the strict sense of the word and we would not expect it to incur a legal penalty. When a lowly Deir el-Medina workman caught his bride-to-be in flagrante delicto with the experienced and wealthy rake Mery-Sekhmet, he reported the matter to the magistrates.[7] Somewhat unexpectedly, the magistrates ordered that the fiancé be punished with 100 blows; as friends of Mery-Sekhmet it seems that they did not appreciate the complaint of an inferior against a social superior. This was clearly unjust, but it was only when one of the foremen took up the 'abomination' that justice prevailed and Mery-Sekhmet was made to swear that he would leave the girl alone, or else face mutilation and exile to Kush.

Mery-Sekhmet, however, did not take his oath seriously and soon the young lady was pregnant. This time Mery-Sekhmet's own father dragged him before the magistrates. Now, in spite of the obvious breach of his earlier promise, the unrepentant lover was again required to swear that he would not go near the lady. What had the wronged fiancé expected the magistrates to do in this case? As the couple were not married at the time of the offence, and were sleeping in separate houses, his right to control the woman's behaviour may well have been limited. It would appear that he was not appealing to the formal *kenbet* for judgement, nor was he seeking to punish or discard his intended. Rather, he was asking the magistrates to intercede informally with their friend Mery-Sekhmet on his behalf.

Diodorus Siculus tells us that the adulterous Egyptian wife was liable to have her nose cut off while her lover received 1000 blows; he cites castration as the punishment for rape.[8] As we have already seen, however, the punishments recorded by Diodorus tend to be over-dramatic and cannot be relied upon. When we turn from fiction and reported history to contemporary documents it seems that divorce, loss of property rights and social disgrace were more likely to follow discovery. Some Late Period marriage contracts even specify 'the great sin that is found in a wife' as grounds for repudiation without financial compensation. While the growing

Greek influence at this time was tending towards ever-increasing restrictions on the behaviour of women, it may not be stretching the evidence too far to imagine a similar financial penalty existing in dynastic times.

Wife-beating, presumably the most common response to infidelity, was considered a private matter and therefore, like all forms of physical aggression, is rarely attested in the legal documentation. Deir el-Medina has yielded only one passing reference to this subject: Ostracon Nash 5 is a badly damaged record which seems to imply that a workman had approached the court on behalf of a beaten woman. The abuser, Amenemope, seems to have been found guilty, but then the text becomes hopelessly confused and we are not sure of the final outcome of the case. An even more oblique reference to the ill-treatment of a wife is a letter primarily concerned with the supply of ointment: 'the woman has run away to the village ... look after her and don't do what you usually have done!'[9] The reason for the ill-treatment is, unfortunately, not given.

Parallels from other societies, both ancient and modern, suggest that the seduction or even rape of an unmarried girl was often followed by a hastily arranged marriage, the avoidance of scandal being of primary concern. In Egypt, however, the more relaxed attitudes towards sex, and indeed childbirth, before marriage may have made such action unnecessary. Rape, like all personal crimes of violence, is seldom reported; this suggests not that it was unknown, but that it was considered to be an entirely private matter. When such matters were brought to the attention of the authorities, action obviously had to be taken to maintain law and order. We therefore find claims made on behalf of Ramesses III that 'I caused the woman of Egypt to go about freely, wheresoever she desired, without a foreigner or anyone else attacking her on the road.'[10]

While women were expected to remain faithful, men were not. Prostitution, although understandably not well represented in the archaeological record, was considered a legitimate trade and the beautiful temptresses of the Turin Erotic Papyrus were surely not the only members of their profession. The scribes did warn young men against consorting with women of easy virtue, but then they advised against anything that might distract the young man from his studies and we have little reason to think that anyone heeded their words.

We have already seen that female domestics might be considered the legitimate sexual partners of their masters; some might even be elevated to the status of concubine and their children included in their father's tomb alongside their legitimate half-siblings. Wives may not have approved, but they seem to have accepted their lot. What was not acceptable, and where Paneb went wrong, was for a man to associate with another man's wife; this was a clear breach of propriety. Nor, it seems, was it acceptable for a married man to behave in an irregular fashion.

In a Twentieth Dynasty letter from Deir el-Medina we read the story of a married man, Nesamenemope, who for eight months has been sleeping with an unnamed woman who is not his wife.[11] The wronged wife's family do not approve of this arrangement and one night they determine to do something about it. An appeal to the court is clearly out of the question – technically, no crime has been committed. Instead, raising a rabble of villagers, they march to the woman's house: 'we are going to beat her, together with her people.' Clearly they hold the woman responsible for the husband's lapse from virtue. Fortunately a steward is able to hold back the crowd before sending a message to the couple. If they are to continue their affair Nesamenemope should first regularise the situation by divorcing his wife, thus providing for her and setting her free to marry another. There is no suggestion that the mistress herself is married, and yet Nesamenemope's callous treatment of his wife is sufficient to enrage his community.

It seems that sexual acts between consenting adults, even if they did not fit into the generally accepted family pattern, were tolerated by society as long as they did no harm to others, although the nuclear family of husband, wife and children was at all times held up as the ideal. Homosexuality was not considered to be a crime, but neither was it expected to be a pleasure. Homosexual rape was a means of degrading the victim, of reducing him to the status of a woman. Thus, when the wicked Seth abuses his nephew he is not just satisfying his own lust, he is submitting Horus to a humiliating, emasculating ordeal:

> Then Seth said to Horus: 'Come, let us have a feast day at my house.' And Horus said to him: 'I will, I will.' Now when evening had come a bed was made for them, and they lay down together. At night, Seth let his member become stiff, and he inserted it between the thighs of Horus. And Horus placed his hand between his thighs and caught the semen of Seth.[12]

Lesbianism goes unrecorded save for a mention in a dream book written for women: 'If she dreams that a woman is having intercourse with her, she will come to a bad end.'[13] Whether this silence conveys total acceptance, or total denial, of female homosexuality is not obvious. The dream books include a number of erotic dreams, many of which concern bestiality, which is also apparently not a crime although it is certainly a moral outrage. The men's dream book, which emphasises the folly of sleeping with a married woman, also mentions the dangers of a man dreaming of copulation with his mother, with his wife in the sun, and with a pig.[14] The woman's dream book details intercourse somewhat improbably with a whole zoo of animals including a mouse, a serpent and a crocodile. All of these are classed as bad signs. They are, however, just dreams. Where bestiality does get mentioned in the court it is in the form of a curse: 'may a donkey **** you and your wife!'

# CHAPTER 12

# THE LAST JUDGEMENT

A criminal might successfully evade detection in the world of the living. After death, however, there could be no escape from divine judgement. As the scribe Any recognised: 'He who sins by falsehood, afterwards the god finds out the righteous man, when his fate has come to seize him.'[1]

In *Setne 2* is the story of Setne's beloved son, Si-Osiri, a gifted magician who is able to take his father on a visit to the shadowy land of the dead. Here Setne is shown the fiendish punishments reserved for the wicked. In the fourth hall he comes across men being tortured with perpetual hunger and thirst; the food and drink they crave is suspended just out of reach and, as they struggle upwards, others dig pits at their feet. In the same hall are those condemned constantly to plait ropes which are immediately chewed apart by donkeys. Passing through the fifth and sixth halls, Setne reaches the seventh, where:

> He saw the mysterious form of the great god Osiris, seated on a throne of finest gold and wearing his crown. The great god Anubis was on his left, and the great god Thoth was on his right. The gods of the tribunal stood both to his left and right. Before them, in the centre, stood the balance. Here they weighed the good deeds against the misdeeds. Those found to have committed more bad deeds than good are

handed over to the Devourer, who belongs to the Lord of the Afterlife. Their Bas are destroyed together with their bodies, and they are not allowed to breath ever again.[2]

Setne's tale was written during the Late Period, and his afterlife is clearly tainted with the Greek image of Hades as a place of divine retribution, where Tantalus and Sisyphus suffer perpetual torment. The pure Egyptian Kingdom of Osiris, as seen during the New Kingdom, was somewhat different, with a clear cut-off between those permitted to enter the Kingdom and those barred for ever. Osiris sought to identify those who had led a virtuous rather than a pious earthly life and to exclude the impure in heart. However, by now the route to the afterlife had been so well mapped, the questions Osiris and his minions would pose so well documented, that the wealthy could die fairly confident of achieving entry. As long as they had not so offended on earth that their mortal remains were destroyed, they were virtually certain to find their way to the Field of Reeds.

The ceremonies of death were well understood. The corpse, suitably mummified and fortified with sacred charms, would be laid to rest in the tomb accompanied by the magical texts which would act as a guidebook to the afterlife. Then, all rituals over, all lights extinguished, the deceased was left alone so that the long journey of the soul might begin. To the Egyptians the soul was a tripartite entity, taking the form of three distinct yet closely related spirits which would, at the time of death, be freed from the body. For there to be any hope of eternal life all three of these spirits must survive beyond death. It perhaps goes without saying that it is very difficult to provide a precise definition of the Egyptian spirits in modern terms, as many of the more subtle nuances of ancient understanding are now irretrievably lost. However, bearing this limitation in mind, we may classify the Ba as the spirit of personality, the Ka as the spirit of life, and the Akh as the spirit of immortality.

After death the Ka needed to remain at all times close to the body; it was thus vulnerable to the decay of the corpse and dependent on the living for provision of the food and drink needed for its survival. The Ba, conventionally depicted as a human-headed bird, enjoyed a less restricted existence; it made its home in the tomb and yet was free to pay brief visits to the land of the living. Only the Akh had the freedom to leave the tomb for ever. The Akh could, depending upon the beliefs of the deceased, shine among the night stars, sail by day in the solar barque of Re or, a popular New Kingdom choice, dwell for ever with Osiris in the Field of Reeds.

The Field was a truly wonderful place, the flawless mirror image of living Egypt complete with flowing river, fertile fields and even a social hierarchy topped by a dead rather than a living king. It is this perfect immortal kingdom, rather than the flawed mortal Egypt, that adorns the painted Theban tomb of Sennedjem which acted as our introduction to this book.

> Hail, daughter of Anubis, above the hatches of heaven, Companion of Thoth above the ladder's rails. Open Unas's path, let Unas pass.
> Hail, Ostrich on the twisting water's shore. Open Unas's path, let Unas pass.
>
> *From the Pyramid text of King Unas*[3]

First, however, the Akh faced a journey that was both long and perilous. Passing over the western horizon, constantly following the setting sun, the spirit travelled onwards until it came to a magical maze, a labyrinth of gates and doors. Here, to gain entrance, it faced a relentless cross-questioning from both the doorkeepers and the doors themselves. It was essential that the spirit address its tormentors by name, as knowledge of a personal name conferred power over an individual; and it was fortunate that guidebooks to the afterlife, listing these names, could legitimately be buried with the deceased.

The form of these guidebooks evolved as the dynasties progressed. The Old Kingdom Pharaohs had been provided with the Pyramid Texts, a series of spells that would protect only the dead king. The more democratic Middle Kingdom passport to the afterlife took the form of spells and incantations, the Coffin Texts, which, as their modern name suggests, were conveniently painted on the insides of the rectangular wooden coffins used to bury the wealthier members of society:

> the first room: the secret room of she who possesses beer jars before the god.
> The second room: the room of . . . mistress of the blessed.
> The third room: the room of the great lady, mistress of the shrine, whom Re knows in his boat.
> The fourth room: the room of the fiery one, lady of punishment, the protectress who gives bread to those who are on their bellies.
> The fifth room: the room of the lady of life, mistress of provisions, who nourishes the gods.
> The sixth room: the room of Maat, lady of the house of the Horizon . . .
> The seventh room: the room of she who is hidden, mistress of the paths.[4]
>
> *Middle Kingdom spell for proceeding to the gates and to those*
> *who are in charge of the gate of the tomb*

Chaos was a constant threat to the Egyptian, even when dead. It was known that normality could be overturned by death, and so we find spells specifically designed to ensure the continuity of 'rightness'. The coffin spells, for example, include incantations to prevent the deceased from being upside down, and from having to eat faeces and drink urine.

During the New Kingdom an illuminated papyrus scroll, inscribed with *The Chapters of Coming Forth by Day*, or the *Book of the Dead*, guaranteed a safe passage to eternity. By now the judgement of the dead forms the most important element in the after-death journey, with a divine tribunal judging the whole life of the deceased in an impressive court-room drama. Having safely navigated the magical maze, the spirit would enter into the Hall of Judgement where the forty-two assessor-gods waited. Here, before King Osiris himself, the deceased was given the opportunity to justify his or her mortal life by reciting the so-called 'negative confession' – less a confession than a standard list of moral and ethical crimes which he or she claimed not to have committed. These included murder, theft, greed, taking advantage of the poor and weak, stealing milk from babies, causing fear and pain, adultery and sexual deviance, lying, spying, manipulating weights and measures, violence and arrogance, offences against the king and offences against the gods.

As in the tomb inscriptions discussed in Chapter 1, the emphasis here is very much on the avoidance of sin rather than the active pursuit of virtue, although the denials of wrongdoing are followed by a brief affirmation of adherence to the correct way of life. Specific, individual sins are entirely excluded; perhaps it was considered too dangerous to allow Osiris to judge each person as a unique, flawed individual, or maybe the expense and practicalities of preparing a separate list of sins for each person were just too great. Instead, the dead went to the grave with a general list of offences compiled to suit all Egyptians. As such, the *Book of the Dead* provides a good insight into society's view of acceptable and unacceptable behaviour:[5] 'I have not made anyone miserable, nor have I made anyone weep. I have not killed anyone, nor have I ordered that anyone be killed . . . I have not copulated unlawfully.'

The dramatic climax to the trial is depicted in the Nineteenth Dynasty papyrus of Hunefer.[6] The jackal-headed Anubis steps forward to weigh the heart of the deceased against the feather of

Maat, the symbol of truth and justice which here serves as the ethical standard.[7] Thoth, the divine ibis-headed scribe, is present to pronounce the verdict and record it in his scroll, while close by lurks Ammit, 'Eater of the Dead', a slavering monster endowed with the head of a crocodile, the foreparts of a lion and the hindparts of a hippopotamus. There is always the danger that the heart might speak out against the deceased; fortunately, spells were specifically designed to avert such a calamity:

> O my heart which I had from my mother, O my heart which
> I had on earth, do not rise up against me as a witness in the
> presence of the Lord of Things; do not speak against me
> saying what I have done; do not bring up against me
> anything I have done in the presence of the Great God, Lord
> of the West.
>
> Book of the Dead, *spell 30, often found engraved on the heart scarab*

The vindicated, those proved to be truly light of heart, will be transfigured to become the blessed dead, gaining immediate admittance to the Field of Reeds. Those whose hearts are heavy meet an awful fate: their hearts thrown to Ammit, they cannot be transfigured and are henceforth doomed to haunt the living as malevolent, restless ghosts.

From the Old Kingdom onwards we find the idea that the recently dead, always touchy and quick to take offence, might wish to harm the living. A handful of personal letters addressed to the dead testifies to the extent to which the deceased were believed capable of interfering in mortal affairs. Otherwise inexplicable vexations – illnesses, deaths, bad luck – might be blamed on evil spirits, and in some of their letters the living plead for an end to their persecution.

Not all the dead were hostile, however, and occasionally the ghost is accorded a role that might more conventionally have been given to the court or the oracle. A letter written by a widow to her recently deceased husband informs him that his relations have stolen the property which she considers should rightly have passed to herself and her son, and she expects him to exert his influence to right this wrong: 'But now here is Uabuet, who has come with Isesi to devastate your house. She has taken everything that was there to enrich Isesi and to impoverish your son. How could your heart remain indifferent to this matter?'[8] She even expects him to enlist his dead father in his campaign. Whether this letter was written instead of, or after, a (presumably failed) legal case we will never know, although it seems clear that where a case rested on weak legal grounds the intervention of a ghost was seen as an effective means of ensuring that justice was done to the otherwise unprotected.

If it was possible to live after death, it had to be possible to die again. Dying the Second Death, the descent into permanent oblivion, was a truly terrible fate, and spells 'for not perishing in the land of the dead' are included in tombs from the Old Kingdom onwards. This very real fear made the infliction of the Second Death a suitably awful punishment for those who had committed the most unforgivable of crimes. But how to kill one who was already dead? Essentially, the Second Death was caused by the destruction of the corpse. This would lead directly to the death of the Ka; the death of the Ba and the Akh would soon follow.

Not unnaturally, anything that caused the destruction of the body was feared, and the stories that tell of unfortunates being burned, eaten by dogs or snatched by crocodiles are intended to convey a horror beyond death itself. Fortunately, it was understood that, in an emergency, the Ka could survive in a statue, a portrait, a written name or even a memory. This theological principle was of little comfort to the poor and illiterate who made up the bulk of Egypt's population and who had little or no chance of preserving their own image. At the other end of the social scale, however, we find successive Pharaohs filling Egypt with their own images in a desperate attempt to ensure that their names would live for ever. This was not mere vanity. The kings knew that if they were ever forgotten by the living they would die for ever.

On at least one occasion during the New Kingdom the imposition of the Second Death was taken a stage further, with a serious attempt being made to delete all memory of the deceased from Egypt's history. The *damnatio memoriae* was a time-consuming, expensive and labour-intensive task. As such, it was reserved for the greatest of royal offenders: Akhenaten and his closest followers.

Traditionally the post-mortem erasure of Hatchepsut's name and image has been interpreted as a typical *damnatio memoriae*, a spiteful gesture by a vengeful Tuthmosis III, the rightful king who had been denied his solo reign for some twenty-two years. However, the facts do not quite fit this interpretation. Archaeological evidence has proved that the attack on Hatchepsut's memory was both delayed and incomplete. While it is possible to imagine Tuthmosis wishing to avenge himself on his stepmother, it is very difficult to imagine him waiting some twenty years before giving way to his emotion. Nor is it easy to imagine Egypt's greatest general allowing his workers to carry out his commands with such complete inefficiency; Hatchepsut's name and image were by no means totally removed from her monuments and may still be seen today. It seems that the attacks on Hatchepsut's memory were less an attempt to deny the female Pharaoh eternal life than a more mercenary attempt to hijack her achievements and monuments. Hatchepsut's reign fell entirely within the reign of Tuthmosis III; he may have felt it entirely reasonable to delete all reference to his co-regent, gaining in the process sole credit for the joint reign.

The *damnatio memoriae* executed against Akhenaten and his court some 150 years later was a very different matter. The death of Akhenaten had seen the death of his innovative monotheistic religion and a quiet resumption of the old ways. Soon, however, there came a determined attempt to erase all trace of the 'great criminal of Akhetaten [Amarna]', Akhenaten's unforgivable offence being the rejection of the traditional state gods and a challenging of the official image of kingship. Now, throughout Egypt, Akhenaten's name, image and monuments were to be erased, defaced and torn down. The city of Amarna was substantially dismantled and not one of Akhenaten's Theban monuments survived the onslaught.

At Thebes, however, many of Akhenaten's building blocks were preserved as fill inside the later walls and gateways of the Karnak temple. Horemheb's second pylon included many inscribed blocks taken from Queen Nefertiti's *Hwt Benben* temple. Hidden from view within the pylon, Horemheb's workmen had carefully reassembled the blocks to reconstruct partial scenes, at least two of which were built upside-down and several of which were defaced. The persecution of Akhenaten's memory lasted well into the reign of Ramesses II, when Egypt's historians decreed that the reigns of Akhenaten, Smenkhkare, Tutankhamen and Ay had never occurred. From this time on the official king lists jumped from Amenhotep III to Horemheb.

Akhenaten, denied his own name, was now known as 'the great criminal'. He was by no means the only Egyptian to lose the use of his own name. All Egyptian personal names had a meaning, and where the accused bore a blatantly inappropriate name it might be changed by the court scribes into something more suitable. In the Ramesses III regicide trials, for example, we find Mersure, 'Re-loves-him', renamed Mesedsure 'Re-hates-him'. Whether this should be seen as a form of de-baptism, an attempt to destroy all earthly memory of the accused by denying his right to his given name, or as a more practical response to the problem of involving a god, no matter how peripherally, in a serious court case, is not clear.

# NOTES

## INTRODUCTION: LAW IN ACTION, *pages 3–15*

1 From the Middle Kingdom Maxims of the scribe Ptah-hotep.
2 Diodorus Siculus, *Histories*, I.75. This and all subsequent quotations from Diodorus are adapted from the translation by C. H. Oldfather and C. L. Sherman, Loeb Classical Library (London and New York, 1933–67).
3 G. Mattha, *The Demotic Legal Code of Hermopolis West* (Cairo, 1975).
4 Diodorus Siculus, *Histories*, I.76.
5 From the *Instruction of Ankhsheshonq*. For a translation of this text with commentary see M. Lichtheim, *Ancient Egyptian Literature* (Berkeley, 1973–80), III, 159–84.
6 For a full translation of this story see Lichtheim, *Ancient Egyptian Literature*, I, 169–84. R. O. Faulkner's translation of this tale is given in W. K. Simpson (ed.), *The Literature of Ancient Egypt: An Anthology of Stories, Instructions and Poetry* (New Haven and London, 1973), pp. 31–49.

## CHAPTER 1: MAAT AND THE KING, *pages 16–33*

1 For a full translation see M. Lichtheim, *Ancient Egyptian Literature* (Berkeley, 1973–80), II, 197–9.
2 Extract from the Middle Kingdom Admonitions of Ipuwer. For a

full translation see Lichtheim, *Ancient Egyptian Literature*, I, 149–63.

3 For these and similar texts see M. Lichtheim, *Maat in Egyptian Autobiographies and Related Studies* (Gottingen, 1992).

4 Extracts from the *Instructions of Amenemope*. For a full translation see Lichtheim, *Ancient Egyptian Literature*, II, 146–63.

5 Middle Kingdom text describing the role of kingship. See J. Assmann, 'Der König als Sonnenpriester: Ein kosmographischer Begleittext zur kultischen Sonnenhymnik', *Abhandlungen des Deutschen Archäologischen Instituts, Abteilung Kairo*, 7 (1970), 17–22.

6 Extract from the restoration stela of Tutankhamen, quoted and discussed in A. Gardiner, *Egypt of the Pharaohs* (Oxford, 1961), pp. 236–7. See also Chapter 7, note 2.

7 Extract from the Speos Artemidos inscription of Hatchepsut, discussed in J. A. Tyldesley, *Hatchepsut: The Female Pharaoh* (London, 1996), pp. 157–9.

8 These scenes are discussed in detail in E. S. Hall, *The Pharaoh Smites his Enemies* (Berlin, 1986).

9 The scanty post-dynastic evidence for human sacrifice has been summarised by J. G. Griffiths, 'Human Sacrifices in Egypt: The Classical Evidence', *Annales du Service des Antiquités de l'Egypte*, 48 (1948), 409–23.

10 Diodorus Siculus, *Histories*, I.88.

11 Plutarch, *De Iside et Osiride*, 73.

12 Achilles Tatius, III.15, describing the murderous and cannibalistic rites of the Egyptian Boukoloi in AD 171. This translation adapted from R. Alston, 'The Revolt of the Boukoloi: Geography, History and Myth', in K. Hopwood (ed.), *Organised Crime in Antiquity* (London, 1999), pp. 129–53.

13 Discussed in more detail in A. Grimm, 'Ein Käfig für einen Gefangenen in einem Ritual zur Vernichtung von Feiden', *Journal of Egyptian Archaeology*, 73 (1987), 202–6.

14 Old Kingdom execration text. This translation after E. Bresciani,

'Foreigners', in S. Donadoni (ed.), *The Egyptians*, trans. R. Bianchi *et al.* (Chicago and London, 1997), p. 222.

15 Translation after D. Lorton, 'The Treatment of Criminals in Ancient Egypt through the New Kingdom', *Journal of the Economic and Social History of the Orient*, 20:1 (1977), 6.

16 Lorton, p. 11.

17 F. Ll. Griffith, 'The Abydos Decree of Seti I at Nauri', *Journal of Egyptian Archaeology*, 13 (1927), 193–208.

18 Lichtheim, *Ancient Egyptian Literature*, II, 52–7.

19 K. Pflüger, 'The Edict of King Horemhab', *Journal of Near Eastern Studies*, 5:1 (1946), 260–76.

20 This case is discussed in K. A. Kitchen, *Pharaoh Triumphant: The Life and Times of Ramesses II* (Warminster, 1982), pp. 133–5.

## CHAPTER 2: THE VIZIER: UPHOLDER OF JUSTICE, *pages 34–46*

1 Text from the tomb of Amenemhet (TT 82). For a full translation with commentary and references see M. Lichtheim, *Maat in Egyptian Autobiographies and Related Studies* (Gottingen, 1992), pp. 54–6.

2 For a full translation with a detailed commentary and a discussion of the role of the vizier see G. P. F. van der Boorn, *The Duties of the Vizier: Civil Administration in the Early New Kingdom* (London and New York, 1988).

3 From the New Kingdom Instructions of Amenemope. M. Lichtheim, *Ancient Egyptian Literature* (Berkeley, 1973–80), II, 146–63.

4 For a full translation see W. K. Simpson (ed.), *The Literature of Ancient Egypt: An Anthology of Stories, Instructions and Poetry* (New Haven and London, 1973), pp. 180–92.

5 From the Middle Kingdom *Satire of the Trades*. For a full translation of this text see Simpson, pp. 329–36.

6 From the Old Kingdom Autobiography of Weni. Lichtheim, *Ancient Egyptian Literature*, I, 18–23. During the New Kingdom

the army developed into a more professional organisation and there was no need to enforce national service.

7 Discussed in T. G. H. James, *Pharaoh's People: Scenes from Life in Imperial Egypt* (Oxford, 1984), p. 87.

8 W. C. Hayes, *A Papyrus of the Late Middle Kingdom in the Brooklyn Museum* (Brooklyn, 1955). All subsequent extracts from this papyrus are adapted from this translation.

9 Papyrus Lansing. Translation after Lichtheim, *Ancient Egyptian Literature*, II, 172.

10 For a full translation see James, pp. 60–1.

11 A. H. Gardiner, *The Inscription of Mes: A Contribution to the Study of Egyptian Judicial Procedure* (Leipzig, 1905).

## CHAPTER 3: OFFICERS OF THE LAW, *pages 47–59*

1 N. de G. Davies *The Rock Tombs of el-Amarna, 4: The Tombs of Penthu, Mahu and Others*, (London, 1906). The quotation is from p. 18.

2 J. Cerny, *A Community of Workmen at Thebes in the Ramesside Period*, (Cairo, 1973), pp. 277–8.

3 The Instructions of Djehuty-mes. Quoted and discussed in A. G. McDowell, *Jurisdiction in the Workmen's Community at Thebes* (Leiden, 1990), p. 44.

4 Ostracon Oriental Institute 12073. Discussed in Cerny, pp. 282–3; McDowell, pp. 180–1.

5 From the Admonitions of Ipuwer. For a full translation see M. Lichtheim, *Ancient Egyptian Literature* (Berkeley, 1973–80), I, 149–63.

6 Genesis 41:46–57.

7 Figures quoted by B. J. Kemp, *Ancient Egypt: Anatomy of a Civilization*, (London and New York, 1989), p. 192.

8 Letter quoted in K. A. Kitchen, *Pharaoh Triumphant: The Life and Times of Ramesses II*, (Warminster, 1982), pp. 131–2.

9 Lichtheim, *Ancient Egyptian Literature*, I, 168–75.

10 N. de G. Davies, *The Rock Tombs of Deir el Gebrawi, 1: Tomb of*

*Aba and Smaller Tombs of the Southern Group*, (London, 1902), p. 33.

11 Translated and discussed in Lichtheim, *Ancient Egyptian Literature*, I, 61–80.

12 These two cases are discussed in McDowell, pp. 226–7. We will meet the notorious Paneb again in Chapters 9 and 11.

13 J. Gardiner Wilson, *The Ancient Egyptians: Their Life and Customs* (London, 1836; rev. abridged ed., 1988), II, 210.

14 From the Admonitions of Ipuwer. For a full translation see Lichtheim, *Ancient Egyptian Literature*, I, 149–63.

CHAPTER 4: CRIMES AND PUNISHMENTS, *pages 60–76*

1 Diodorus Siculus, *Histories* I.77.

2 J. Cerny, 'Restitution of, and Penalty Attaching to, Stolen Property in Ramesside Times', *Journal of Egyptian Archaeology*, 23:2 (1937), 186–9. Cerny discusses both this case and the case of Lute cited below.

3 Ostracon Turin 57455. Translation after A. G. McDowell, *Jurisdiction in the Workmen's Community of Deir el-Medina* (Leiden, 1990), p. 231.

4 For a full translation of this tale see M. Lichtheim, *Ancient Egyptian Literature* (Berkeley, 1973–80), II, 211–14; E. F. Wente in W. K. Simpson (ed.), *The Literature of Ancient Egypt: An Anthology of Stories, Instructions and Poetry* (New Haven and London, 1973), pp. 127–32.

5 Quoted in D. Lorton, 'The Treatment of Criminals in Ancient Egypt', in J. M. Sasson (ed.), *The Treatment of Criminals in the Ancient Near East* (Leiden, 1977), p. 27.

6 The evidence concerning this form of execution is reviewed in detail in M. A. Leahy, 'Death by Fire in Ancient Egypt', *Journal of the Economic and Social History of the Orient*, 27:2 (1984), 199–206.

7 The cycle of stories is translated by W. K. Simpson under the title 'King Cheops and the Magicians' in Simpson (ed.), pp. 15–30. The translation of the words 'he placed fire on her' is crucial to this

interpretation, but there seems little reason to support the suggestion that this phrase refers to branding rather than death; see Lorton, pp. 2–64.

8 The Abydos stela of Neferhotep and Ostracon Nash 2 are discussed in both Lorton and Leahy. The Tod Inscription of Senwosret I is discussed in H. Willems, 'Crime, Cult and Capital Punishment', *Journal of Egyptian Archaeology*, 76 (1990), 41.

9 R. Caminos, *The Chronicle of Prince Osorkon*, (Rome, 1954).

10 For a full translation with commentary see Lichtheim, *Ancient Egyptian Literature*, III, 159–84.

11 Extract from the Turin Judicial Papyrus. For a full translation consult A. J. Peden, *Egyptian Historical Inscriptions of the Twentieth Dynasty* (Jonsered, 1994), pp. 195–210.

12 Discussed in detail by Nick Fisher when considering the case of classical Athens; see N. Fisher, 'Workshop of Villains: Was There Much Organised Crime in Classical Athens?' in K. Hopwood (ed.), *Organised Crime in Antiquity* (London, 1999), pp. 53–96: 63.

13 But see the discussion of the Demenjibtawy decree in Chapter 1.

14 Translations of this crucial passage vary. See, for example, R. O. Faulkner in Simpson (ed.), pp. 180–92; Lichtheim, *Ancient Egyptian Literature*, I, 97–109.

15 From the Middle Kingdom Loyalist Instruction on the Sehetepi-bre funerary stela. For W. K. Simpson's translation of this text see Simpson (ed.), pp. 198–200.

16 Translation after R. O. Faulkner, *The Ancient Egyptian Coffin Texts*, Vol. 1 (Warminster, 1973), pp. 269–72.

17 Translation after R. O. Faulkner, *The Ancient Egyptian Coffin Texts*, Vol. 2 (Warminster, 1977), pp. 48–9.

18 This case has been discussed in Chapter 3. A statue of Tuthmosis III in the Louvre (E.11673) may also contain an oblique reference to beating as a punishment. This is discussed in G. P. F. van den Boorn, *The Duties of the Vizier: Civil Administration in the Early New Kingdom* (London and New York, 1988), pp. 85–6.

19 Ostracon Deir el-Medina 433. Quoted in McDowell, p. 7.

20 Extract from the Twentieth Dynasty Papyrus BM 10052. Translation after T. E. Peet, *The Great Tomb-Robberies of the Twentieth Egyptian Dynasty* (Oxford, 1930), pp. 147–8.

21 See J. Capart, A. H. Gardiner, and B. van de Walle, 'New Light on the Ramesside Tomb-Robberies', *Journal of Egyptian Archaeology*, 22:2 (1936), 172. 'Twisting' is discussed in Peet, p. 21.

### Chapter 5: Loss of Liberty, *pages 77–88*

1 Ostracon Berlin 12654. Discussed in A. G. McDowell, *Jurisdiction in the Workmen's Community of Deir el-Medina* (Leiden, 1990), p. 232.

2 Papyrus Salt 124. J. Cerny, 'Papyrus Salt 124 (British Museum 10055)', *Journal of Egyptian Archaeology*, 15 (1929), 246.

3 Translation after D. Lorton, 'The Treatment of Criminals in Ancient Egypt', in J. M. Sasson (ed.), *The Treatment of Criminals in the Ancient Near East* (Leiden, 1977), p. 20.

4 Exodus 5:13–14.

5 K. A. Kitchen, *Pharaoh Triumphant: The Life and Times of Ramesses II* (Warminster, 1982), pp. 49–50.

6 El-Lahun Papyri, table 34.17ff. Quoted and discussed in A. Loprieno 'Slaves', in S. Donadoni (ed.), *The Egyptians*, trans. R. Bianchi *et al.* (Chicago and London, 1997), p. 200.

7 As sworn in the court case of Mose, already discussed in Chapter 1. The back of the house included the private area reserved for the man of the house, his womenfolk, children and servants, and the kitchen.

8 A. H. Gardiner, 'The Tomb of Amenemhet, High Priest of Amon', *Zeitschrift für Ägyptische Sprache und Altertumskunde*, 47 (1910), 87–99.

9 See A. Gardiner, 'Adoption Extraordinary', *Journal of Egyptian Archaeology*, 26 (1945), 23–9.

10 Kitchen, p. 138.

11 Quoted and discussed in J. A. Tyldesley, *Ramesses: Egypt's Greatest Pharaoh*, (London, 2000). See also K. A. Kitchen, *Ramesside*

*Inscriptions Translated and Annotated, 2: Ramesses II, Royal Inscriptions* (Oxford, 1996), pp. 86–96.

12 Extract adapted from the Year 5 Libyan war inscription of Ramesses III after A. J. Peden, *Egyptian Historical Inscriptions of the Twentieth Dynasty* (Jonsered, 1994), pp. 7–22.

13 Extract from Papyrus Lansing. See M. Lichtheim, *Ancient Egyptian Literature* (Berkeley, 1973–80), II, 168–75.

14 Papyrus Harris. Quoted in A. E.-M. Bakir, *Slavery in Pharaonic Egypt* (Cairo, 1978), pp. 109–10.

15 Quoted in D. B. Redford, *Egypt, Canaan and Israel in Ancient Times* (Princeton and Cairo, 1992), p. 223. Redford discusses the fate of prisoners-of-war in some detail.

## CHAPTER 6: REGICIDE: THE ULTIMATE REBELLION,
### *pages 89–101*

1 Amarna Letter EA 4. For a full translation see W. L. Moran, *The Amarna Letters* (Baltimore and London, 1992).

2 For a full translation of this text see M. Lichtheim, *Ancient Egyptian Literature,* (Berkeley, 1973–80), II, 135–46.

3 Herodotus, *Histories*, II.107.

4 Extract from the autobiography of Weni as quoted in J. A. Tyldesley, *Daughters of Isis: Women of Ancient Egypt* (London, 1994), p. 189. For a full translation of this text with commentary see Lichtheim, *Ancient Egyptian Literature*, I, 18–22.

5 For a full translation of this text see Lichtheim, *Ancient Egyptian Literature*, I, 135–9.

6 For a full translation of this story see W. K. Simpson in W. K. Simpson (ed.), *The Literature of Ancient Egypt: An Anthology of Stories, Instructions and Poetry* (New Haven and London, 1973), pp. 57–74.

7 Extract from Papyrus Rollin. Translation after that given in H. Goedicke, 'Was Magic Used in the Harem Conspiracy against Ramesses III?', *Journal of Egyptian Archaeology*, 49 (1963), 71–92.

8 See the discussion of this form of killing in Chapter 1. Goedicke,

however, in the article cited above, suggests that the reference to spells and wax models should be read as a non-literal figure of speech.

9 This, and all subsequent extracts from the Turin Judicial Papyrus, are based on that suggested by A. J. Peden, *Egyptian Historical Inscriptions of the Twentieth Dynasty*, (Jonsered, 1994), pp. 195–210.

10 This is discussed further in A. de Buck, 'The Judicial Papyrus of Turin', *Journal of Egyptian Archaeology*, 23:2 (1937), 152–64.

## CHAPTER 7: TUTANKHAMEN: A MURDER MYSTERY?
### pages 102–10

1 The first suggestion that Tutankhamen may have been murdered was made by A. C. Mace, 'The Egyptian Expedition 1922–23', *Bulletin of the Metropolitan Museum of Art*, 18:2 (1923), 6. For a more recent and far more detailed exploration of the murder theory see B. Brier, *The Murder of Tutankhamen: A 3000 Year Old Murder Mystery* (London, 1998). Brier scrupulously states that the evidence he presents is not absolute proof of murder, but the title of his book seems to have persuaded many of his readers otherwise.

2 Extract from the restoration stela of Tutankhamen at Karnak. For a full translation of this text see B. G. Davies, *Egyptian Historical Records of the Later Eighteenth Dynasty, Fascicle VI* (Warminster, 1995), pp. 30–3.

3 There is a vast amount of published literature on the Amarna period. See for example C. Aldred *Akhenaten: King of Egypt* (London, 1988); D. B. Redford, *Akhenaten: The Heretic King* (Princeton, 1984); J. A. Tyldesley, *Nefertiti: Egypt's Sun Queen* (London, 1998). All these books provide extensive bibliographies.

4 Translation after H. G. Guterbock, as quoted in A. R. Schulman, 'Ankhesenamun, Nofretity and the Amka Affair', *Journal of the American Research Centre in Egypt*, 15 (1978), 43–8. This article discusses the identity of the letter-writer in detail.

5 For a discussion of the 'scientific' mistreatment of Tutankhamen's mummy see D. Forbes, 'Abusing Pharaoh', *KMT*, (1992). This article is reprinted in C. Frayling, *The Face of Tutankhamen* (London, 1992), pp. 285–92. Forbes supports the accident hypothesis.

6 Brier, p. 173.

7 For a full translation see J. H. Breasted, *The Edwin Smith Surgical Papyrus* (Chicago, 1930).

## CHAPTER 8: THE SECOND OLDEST PROFESSION, *pages 111–26*

1 Translation after M. Lichtheim, *Ancient Egyptian Literature* (Berkeley, 1973–80), I, 149–63. For an alternative version of this text see R. O. Faulkner in W. K. Simpson (ed.), *The Literature of Ancient Egypt: An Anthology of Stories, Instructions and Poetry* (New Haven and London, 1973), pp. 210–29.

2 The Setne stories are told in Lichtheim, *Ancient Egyptian Literature*, III, 125–51.

3 Herodotus, *Histories* II. 89.

4 *Urkunden* I. 23. Quoted and discussed in S. Donadoni, 'The Dead', in S. Donadoni (ed.), *The Egyptians*, trans. R. Bianchi *et al.* (Chicago and London, 1997), p. 272.

5 Translation adapted from that given by H. Willems, 'Crime, Cult and Capital Punishment', *Journal of Egyptian Archaeology*, 76 (1990), 27–54.

6 Herodotus's tale of the wickedness of King Cheops; *Histories*, II. 126.

7 This translation after K. A. Kitchen, *Pharaoh Triumphant: The Life and Times of Ramesses* II (Warminster, 1982), p. 107.

8 These figures are discussed in M. Lehner, *The Complete Pyramids* (London, 1997), p. 224.

9 Ostracon Cairo 25800.

10 Papyrus BM 10052. The economics of private enterprise and theft are discussed in B. J. Kemp, *Ancient Egypt: Anatomy of a Civilization* (London, 1989), pp. 242–6.

CHAPTER 9: THE ROBBERS OF THE WEST BANK, *pages 127–39*

1 Papyrus BM 10055. For a full translation and discussion see J. Cerny, 'Papyrus Salt 124 (British Museum 10055)', *Journal of Egyptian Archaeology*, 15 (1929), 243–58.

2 Letter written by the mayor of western Thebes. Translation adapted from K. A. Kitchen, *Pharaoh Triumphant* (Warminster, 1982), p. 125.

3 For a full translation and commentary on this ostracon see C. J. Eyre, 'A "Strike" Text from the Theban Necropolis', in J. Ruffle *et al.* (eds.), *Glimpses of Ancient Egypt: Studies in Honour of H. W. Fairman* (Warminster, 1979), pp. 80–91.

4 W. F. Edgerton, *Journal of Near Eastern Archaeology*, 10 (1951), 141.

5 Papyrus Meyer B. Translation after C. N. Reeves and R. H. Wilkinson, *The Complete Valley of the Kings: Tombs and Treasures of Egypt's Greatest Pharaohs* (London, 1996), p. 192.

6 Papyrus BM 10053. Translation after T. G. H. James, *Pharaoh's People: Scenes from Life in Imperial Egypt*, (Oxford, 1984), p. 264.

7 After A. J. Peden, *Egyptian Historical Inscriptions of the Twentieth Dynasty* (Jonsered, 1994), pp. 245–57. For the fascinating story of the discovery and restoration of this papyrus, see J. Capart, A. H., Gardiner and B. van de Walle, 'New Light on the Ramesside Tomb-Robberies', *Journal of Egyptian Archaeology*, 22: 2 (1936), 169–93.

8 Papyrus BM 10054. After T. E. Peet, 'Fresh Light on the Tomb-Robberies at Thebes', *Journal of Egyptian Archaeology*, 11 (1925), 43.

9 Papyrus BM 10052. After Peet, p. 46.

10 Papyrus Abbot BM 10221. For a full translation of this text see Peden, pp. 225–44.

11 Papyrus BM 10052. This text is discussed in C. Aldred, 'More Light on the Ramesside Tomb-Robberies', in Ruffle *et al.* (eds.), pp. 92–9. For a full translation see Peden, pp. 271–6.

12 Papyrus BM 10052. Translation after Peet, p. 40.

13 Papyrus Abbot. Peden, pp. 225–44.

14 A. H. Gardiner, 'Political Crime in Ancient Egypt', *Journal of the Manchester Egyptian and Oriental Society* (1912–13), 57–64.

15 Herodotus, *Histories*, II. 169.

CHAPTER 10: THE VILLAGER AND THE ORACLE, *pages 140–52*

1 For an in-depth, highly readable account of the legal affairs of Deir el-Medina see A. G. McDowell, *Jurisdiction in the Workmen's Community of Deir el-Medina* (Leiden, 1990). Many of the cases discussed below are covered in detail, with additional references, by McDowell.

2 From the unpublished Papyrus Turin 1966; Cerny MS 3.649–51. This case is briefly discussed in B. Davies, *Genealogies and Personality Characteristics of the Workmen in the Deir el-Medina Community during the Ramesside Period*, unpublished doctoral thesis, University of Liverpool, 1996.

3 From the votive stela of Neferabu with a hymn to Ptah. Translation after M. Lichtheim, *Ancient Egyptian Literature* (Berkeley, 1973–80), pp. 109–10.

4 See C. Eyre, 'Fate, Crocodiles and the Judgement of the Dead: Some Mythological Allusions in Egyptian literature', *Studien Zur Altägyptischen Kultur*, 4 (1976), 103–14. Eyre also discusses the *Tale of the Doomed Prince*, Papyrus Harris 500. A full translation of this text is given in Lichtheim, *Ancient Egyptian Literature*, II, 200–3.

5 For perhaps the earliest instance of the oracle see J. Baines and R. B. Parkinson, 'An Old Kingdom Record of an Oracle? Sinai Inscription 13', in J. van Dijk (ed.), *Essays on Ancient Egypt in Honour of Herman Te Velde* (Groningen, 1997), pp. 9–27.

6 Translation after P. F. Dorman, *The Monuments of Senenmut: Problems in Historical Methodology* (London, 1988), p. 22.

7 J. Cerny, 'Egyptian Oracles', in R. A. Parker (ed.), *A Saite Oracle*

*Papyrus from Thebes in the Brooklyn Museum* (New York, 1962), p. 42.

8 See J. Cerny, 'Restitution of, and Penalty Attaching to, Stolen Property in Ramesside Times', *Journal of Egyptian Archaeology*, 23: 2 (1937), 186–9.

9 From the New Kingdom Instructions of Amenemope. For a full translation see Lichtheim, *Ancient Egyptian Literature*, II, 146–63.

### CHAPTER 11: SEX CRIMES, *pages 153–63*

1 Translation after J. Cerny, 'Papyrus Salt 124 (British Museum 10055)', *Journal of Egyptian Archaeology*, 15 (1929), 243–58.

2 These cases of fornication with married women are discussed in detail in C. J. Eyre, 'Crime and Adultery in Ancient Egypt', *Journal of Egyptian Archaeology*, 70 (1984), 92–105.

3 The evidence for official polygamy – as opposed to casual sexual relations with lower ranking female members of the household – is almost entirely drawn from the upper and middle classes and cannot automatically be assumed to apply to the peasant communities. The design of the cramped Deir el-Medina houses would appear to confirm that the workmen were not expected to have more than one wife. Marriage in all its aspects is discussed in G. Robins, *Women in Ancient Egypt* (London, 1993), pp. 56–74; J. A. Tyldesley, *Daughters of Isis: Women of Ancient Egypt* (London, 1994), pp. 45–81; B. Waterson, *Women in Ancient Egypt* (Stroud, 1991), pp. 54–72.

4 All three quoted wisdom texts are to be found in full translation in M. Lichtheim, *Ancient Egyptian Literature* (Berkeley, 1973–80).

5 Herodotus, *Histories*, II: 111.

6 For a full translation of this story see Lichtheim, *Ancient Egyptian Literature* II, 203–11.

7 Papyrus Deir el-Medina 27. Discussed in A. G. McDowell, *Jurisdiction in the Workmen's Community of Deir el-Medina*, (Leiden, 1990), pp. 115, 175.

8 Diodorus Siculus, *Histories*, I.78.

9 Papyrus Deir el-Medina 6. Translation after D. Sweeney, 'Friendship and Frustration: A Study in Papyri Deir el-Medina IV-VI', *Journal of Egyptian Archaeology*, 84 (1998), 103.

10 Papyrus Harris 1. Translation after A. J. Peden, *Egyptian Historical Inscriptions of the Twentieth Dynasty* (Jonsered, 1994), pp. 211–24.

11 Discussed with translation in J. J. Janssen, 'Marriage Problems and Public Reactions', in J. Baines *et al.* (eds.), *Pyramid Studies and Other Essays Presented to I. E. S. Edwards* (London, 1988), pp. 134–7.

12 Extract from the New Kingdom story of Horus and Seth. After J. A. Tyldesley, *Daughters of Isis: Women of Ancient Egypt* (London, 1994), p. 65. This story is discussed in L. Manniche, *Sexual Life in Ancient Egypt* (London, 1987), pp. 56–7.

13 Papyrus Carlsberg XIII. A. Volten, *Demotische Traumdeutung* (Copenhagen, 1942).

14 Papyrus Chester Beatty II (BM 10683).

## CHAPTER 12: THE LAST JUDGEMENT, *pages 164–72*

1 Quotation from C. Eyre, 'Fate, Crocodiles and the Judgement of the Dead: Some Mythological Allusions in Egyptian Literature', *Studien zur Altägyptischen Kultur*, 4 (1976), 103–14. Eyre also discusses the *Tale of the Doomed Prince* told above.

2 For a full translation see M. Lichtheim, *Ancient Egyptian Literature*, (Berkeley, 1973–80), III pp. 138–51.

3 A selection of utterances from the Pyramid Texts is given in Lichtheim, *Ancient Egyptian Literature*, I.

4 From Coffin Text spell 901. Translation after R. O. Faulkner, *The Ancient Egyptian Coffin Texts*, Vol. 3 (Warminster, 1978), p. 56.

5 Discussed in M. Lichtheim, *Maat in Egyptian Autobiographies and Related Studies* (Gottingen, 1992), pp. 125–7.

6 See S. Ikram and A. Dobson, *The Mummy in Ancient Egypt* (London, 1998), Plate II.

7 The use of Maat as an ethical standard in the judgement of the

dead is discussed in S. Morenz, *Egyptian Religion*, trans. A. E. Keep (London, 1973), pp. 126–30.

8 A. Gardiner and K. Sethe, *Letters to the Dead* (London, 1928), p. 1.

# CHRONOLOGICAL TABLE

| Years before Christ | CHRONOLOGY | HISTORICAL EVENTS |
|---|---|---|
| 3000 | Archaic Period (Dynasties 1–2) | Unification of Egypt<br>Memphis founded as capital |
| | Old Kingdom (Dynasties 3–6) | Step-pyramid at Sakkara<br><br>Great Pyramid at Giza |
| 2500 | | |
| | First Intermediate Period (Dynasties 7–11) | Rival dynasties at Thebes and Herakleopolis |
| 2000 | Middle Kingdom (Dynasties 12–13) | Theban kings re-unify Egypt<br>Senwosret III builds fortresses in Nubia<br>Last of the great Royal Pyramids built |
| | Second Intermediate Period (Dynasties 14–17) | Hyksos kings in Northern Egypt<br>Theban kings in the South |
| 1500 | New Kingdom (Dynasties 18–20) | Amarna Period<br>Tutankhamen<br>Ramesses II |
| 1000 | Third Intermediate Period (Dynasties 21–25) | Kings at Tanis<br>Nubian kings<br>Assyrian invasion |
| 500 | Late Period (Dynasties 26–31) | Sais becomes capital of Egypt<br>Egypt conquered by Persians<br>Alexander the Great expels Persians |
| | Ptolemaic Period | |
| AD 0 | | Egypt part of Roman Empire |

# BIBLIOGRAPHY

*Contemporary documents*

The books listed below represent some of the best, and most accessible, translations into English of Egyptian literature and classical texts. They provide a first-class introduction for those approaching Egyptology for the first time. All provide detailed references which will be of interest to the more specialised reader.

Davies, B. G., *Historical Records of the Late Eighteenth Dynasty* (Warminster, 1992–5).

Diodorus Siculus, *Bibliotheca Historica*, trans. C. H. Oldfather and C. L. Sherman, Loeb Classical Library (New York, 1933–67).

Herodotus, *The Histories*, trans. A. de Selincourt, rev. with Introduction and Notes by A. R. Burn (London, 1983).

Kitchen, K. A., *Poetry of Ancient Egypt* (Jonsered, 1999).

Lichtheim, M., *Ancient Egyptian Literature*, 3 vols. (Berkeley, 1973–80).

Parkinson, R. B., *Voices from Ancient Egypt* (London, 1991).

Peden, A. J., *Egyptian Historical Inscriptions of the Twentieth Dynasty* (Jonsered, 1994).

Simpson, W. K. (ed.), *The Literature of Ancient Egypt: An Anthology of Stories, Instructions and Poetry* (New Haven and London, 1973).

Strabo, *The Geography of Strabo VII*, trans. H. L. Jones (New York, 1932).

*Background studies*

The following provide a good introduction to dynastic history, setting the scene for crime and punishment.

Allem, T. G., *The Book of the Dead, or Going Forth by Day* (Chicago, 1974).

Baines, J., and J. Malek, *Atlas of Ancient Egypt* (New York, 1980).

Cerny, J., *A Community of Workmen at Thebes in the Ramesside Period* (Cairo, 1973).

Donadoni, S. (ed.), *The Egyptians*, trans. R. Bianchi *et al.* (Chicago and London, 1997).

Edwards, I. E. S., *The Pyramids of Egypt*, rev. edn (London, 1961).

Gardiner, A. H., *Egypt of the Pharaohs* (Oxford, 1961).

Grimal, N., *A History of Ancient Egypt*, trans. I. Shaw (Oxford, 1992).

Harris, J. R. (ed.), *The Legacy of Egypt*, 2nd edn (Oxford, 1971).

James, T. G. H., *Pharaoh's People: Scenes from Life in Imperial Egypt* (Oxford, 1984).

Kemp, B. J., *Ancient Egypt: Anatomy of a Civilization* (London and New York, 1980).

Lehner, M., *The Complete Pyramids* (London, 1997).

Quirke, S., *Ancient Egyptian Religion* (London, 1992).

Redford, D. B., *Egypt, Canaan and Israel in Ancient Times* (Princeton and Cairo, 1992).

Reeves, C. N., and Wilkinson, R. H., *The Complete Valley of the Kings: Tombs and Treasures of Egypt's Greatest Pharaohs* (London, 1996).

Robins, G., *Women in Ancient Egypt* (London, 1993).

Romer, J., *Valley of the Kings* (London, 1981).

Spencer, A. J., *Death in Ancient Egypt* (London, 1982).

Trigger, B. G., *et al.*, *Ancient Egypt: A Social History* (Cambridge, 1983).

Tyldesley, J. A., *Daughters of Isis: Women of Ancient Egypt* (London, 1994).

## Ancient crime and punishment

Abbot, G., *Rack, Rope and Red-Hot Pincers: A History of Torture and Its Instruments* (London, 1993).

Bakir, A. E.-M., *Slavery in Pharaonic Egypt* (Cairo, 1978).

Bedell, E. D., *Criminal Law in the Egyptian Ramesside Period* (Ann Arbor, 1974).

Hall, E. S., *The Pharaoh Smites His Enemies* (Berlin, 1986).

Hopwood, K. (ed.), *Organised Crime in Antiquity* (London, 1999).

Lichtheim, M., *Maat in Egyptian Autobiographies and Related Studies* (Gottingen, 1992).

Manniche, L., *Sexual Life in Ancient Egypt* (London, 1987).

McDowell, A. G., *Jurisdiction in the Workmen's Community of Deir el-Medina* (Leiden, 1990).

Peet, T. E., *The Great Tomb-Robberies of the Twentieth Egyptian Dynasty* (Oxford, 1930).

Sasson, J. M. (ed.), *The Treatment of Criminals in the Ancient Near East* (London, 1977).

Shafer, B. E. (ed.), *Religion in Ancient Egypt: Gods, Myths and Personal Practice* (London, 1991).

Shaw, I., *Egyptian Warfare and Weapons* (Princes Risborough, 1991).

van den Boorn, G. P. F., *The Duties of the Vizier: Civil Administration in the Early New Kingdom* (London, 1988).

## Modern tales of ancient Egyptian crime

Ancient Egypt is growing increasingly popular as a setting for murder mysteries. Those new to the genre might like to start with Agatha Christie's *Death Comes as the End*, the first book of the type, and then progress to the works of Anton Gill and Lauren Hanley.

# INDEX